THE ANIMAL DRAWING BOOK

FOR

KIDS

How to Draw 365 Animals, Step by Step

woo! jr
KiDS activities

Copyright © 2021 Woo! Jr. Kids Activities LLC / Wendy Piersall. All rights reserved.

Woo! Jr. Kids Activities Founder: Wendy Piersall

Art Director/Instructions Writted and Illustrated by: Lilia Garvin

Cover Illustration: Michael Koch | Sleeping Troll Studios www.sleepingtroll.com

Interior Illustration: Avinash Saini

Published by DragonFruit, an imprint of Mango Publishing, a division of Mango Media Inc.

For permission requests, please contact the publisher at:

Mango Publishing Group
2850 Douglas Road, 2nd Floor
Coral Gables, FL 33134 USA
info@mango.bz

For special orders, quantity sales, course adoptions and corporate sales, please email the publisher at sales@mango.bz. For trade and wholesale sales, please contact Ingram Publisher Services at customer.service@ingramcontent.com or +1.800.509.4887.

The Animal Drawing Book for Kids: How to Draw 365 Animals, Step by Step

ISBN: (p) 978-1-64250-639-6

BISAC: JNF006040—JUVENILE NONFICTION / Art / History

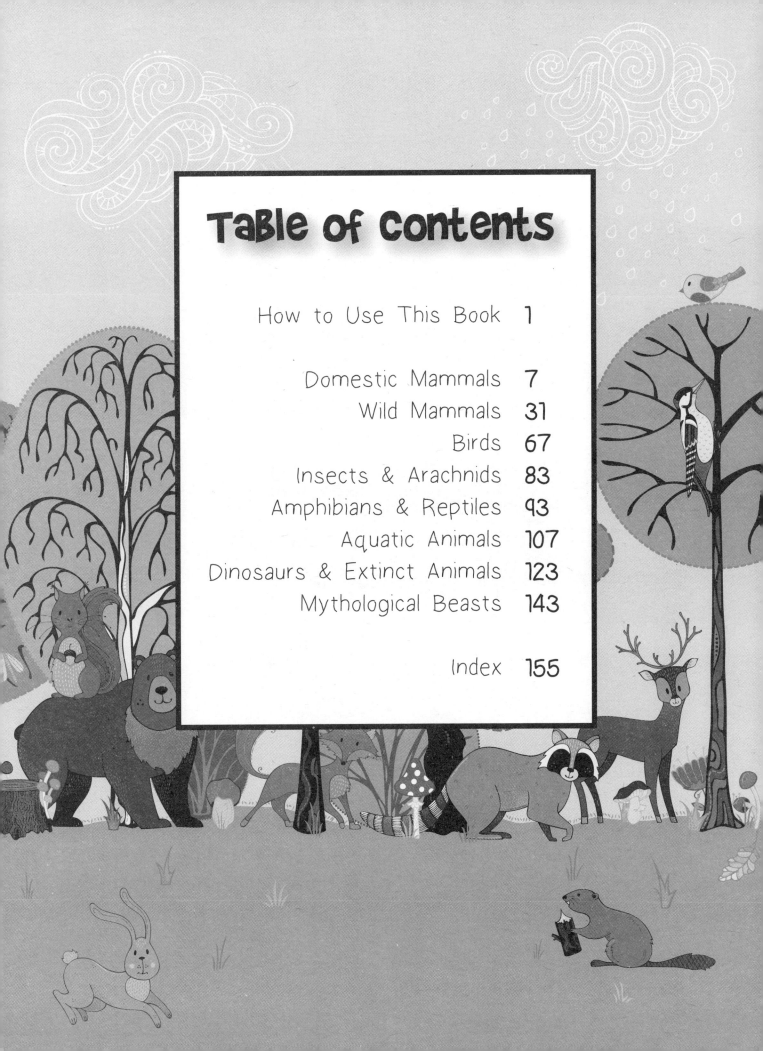

Table of Contents

How to Use This Book!

All you need is a pencil, eraser, and a piece of paper!

Follow each drawing diagram step by step:

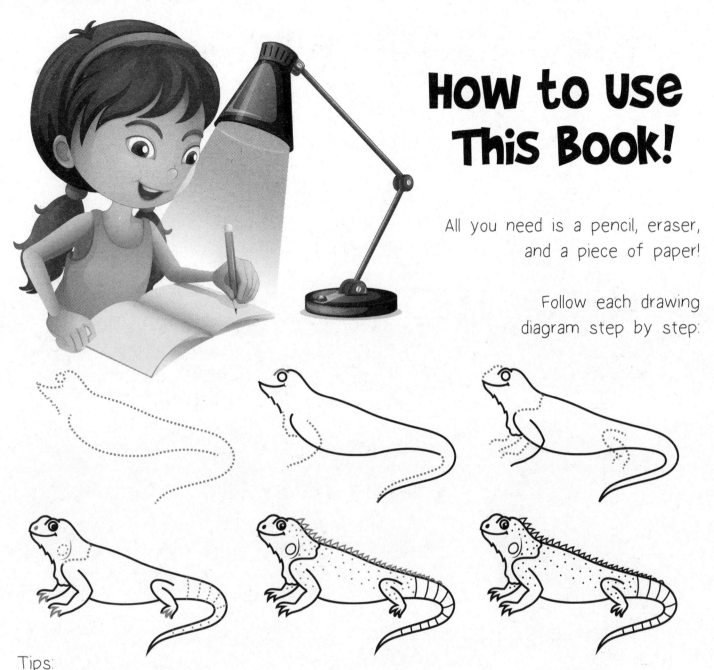

Tips:
Draw lightly at first, because you might need to erase some lines as you work.

Add details according to the diagrams, but don't worry about being perfect! Artists frequently make mistakes – they just find ways to make their mistakes look interesting. You can erase mistakes, or use use them as a new decoration.

Don't worry if your drawings don't turn out quite the way you want them to. Just keep practicing! Sometimes drawing the same thing just a few times will help.

You can draw a new animal every day for 365 days, or several each day. For an extra challenge, use your creativity to combine multiple animals into an entire scene.

Want to add more detail?

You can introduce shading techniques to make your drawings even more realistic and fun! Once you have finished your lines, consider shading in one of these ways:

Shading Technique: Hatching

In hatching, draw lots of lines that don't cross. You can press harder with your pencil to make darker lines, and space them closer together for a more full, consistent gradient (in art, a **gradient** is a transition from one color or shade to another.)

Anywhere you put marks on the paper it will look darker. For your lightest spots, don't put any marks.

Shading Technique: Cross-hatching

Cross-hatching is very similar to hatching. The key difference is that you now also want to make marks coming from a second direction. Practice this technique with pencil or pen. They're both very good materials to cross-hatch with!

Shading Technique: Scumbling

Scumbling is a method where you shade with much more random marks than hatching, or cross-hatching. To scumble, use circular and squiggling marks. Don't worry what direction your pencil is moving in. Try to keep your wrist loose, and relax.

Remember to overlap, or layer, your marks, and put them closer together in your darkest areas.

Shading Technique: Stippling

Stippling is also known as **pointillism**. To stipple, you shade with many, many small dots. This is a bit similar to how pixels are used to shade on a computer screen.

The closeness, or density, of your dots will determine your darkest points. Choose a starting point, and then carefully lift your pencil or pen up, and press down to make your dots. Try to avoid making any lines, or marks.

Shading Technique: Blending

With blending, the marks you make on the paper don't matter as much. You can start with hatched, cross-hatched, or scumbled marks. Try to make your shading smooth, and close together.

Next, rub the pencil marks together. You can use a facial tissue, napkin, or even your fingers. Afterward, make sure to clean your hands when you're done. It's messy!

Practicing Value

Example

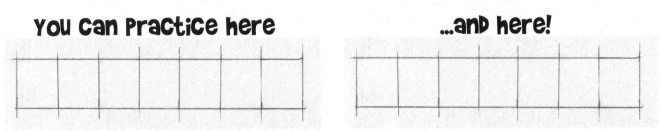

In art, **value** means the degree of lightness or darkness of a color. Right now, since we're shading with pencil, that color is black, and the variation in value is called a **greyscale**. We're going to practice making them.

Use the scale to shade from light to dark. The paper can be your lightest shade. Press a bit harder for each new shade, until you get to the darkest.

You Can Practice here

...and here!

If you want to practice more, you can! First, draw a line of squares. Use a ruler to help you, or any hard surface. It's okay if the lines aren't perfect – then shade!

Step-By-Step Shading

Step 1: Complete your Linework

Find the animal you want to draw by skimming through the book. For this example, we're going to be shading the Akita found on page 14.

Follow the steps to draw your animal, and then make the lines dark by pressing hard with your pencil, or inking over your lines with a pen. If you decide to ink with a pen, wait for the ink to dry and erase the pencil marks underneath.

Step 2: Decide your Method

Let's decide how to shade this good dog. Because our Akita is a furry dog, it looks like hatching would be good at replicating the texture of fur. We're going to hatch lightly with a pencil, to make the Akita's fur look soft. Let's test it out in a small section to see how it looks.

Step 3: Fill in Areas With Shading

Establish which areas you want to be darker on your animal. Here, we've decided to make the top parts of our dog darker, and leave their underside a fluffy white. So, let's introduce more hatching to the other areas we want dark.

Remember to leave some areas paper-white to have highlights, even in your dark spots. It'll make your animals look just a bit more realistic!

Step 4: Add texture to Other Parts

Even though we decided to leave our dog's belly white, we can still go into that area to add some texture. Let's use small marks, and not press very hard. That will make sure the white part of its fur is still light, but add a little bit of dimension to the drawing.

Step 5: Darken your Darks

We've got our lights and our midtones in place. To decide where to put our darkest darks, imagine that a light is shining on our dog and picture in your mind where the shadows would be.

Now, let's take our pencil and add some spots of darker darks to add shadows. We'll gently add tiny bits of shadow to the white areas of fur, layering it in some spots that already have midtones. Careful not to overdo it. Then, we'll bring shadows into the other areas. Darken around the edges, and bring your darkest darks into the areas that have fur shading, leaving those paper-white spots we started with.

Step 6: Last Details

Anything missing still? On our Akita, it looks like we still need to shade its nose and tongue!

Let's do that with small, gentle strokes, keeping carefully inside the area we want to shade. Now, our good dog looks like a finished drawing!

Try it yourself! You can find the **Akita** on page 14.

TiPS & ReMiNDeRS

Varying shading on large areas can add texture to your favorite animals.

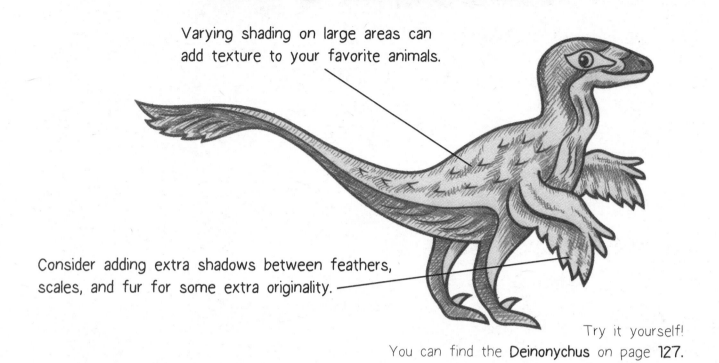

Consider adding extra shadows between feathers, scales, and fur for some extra originality.

Try it yourself!
You can find the **Deinonychus** on page 127.

• •

You can ink your lines and erase the pencil marks beneath before shading.

Leave the paper blank, or use an eraser for highlights.

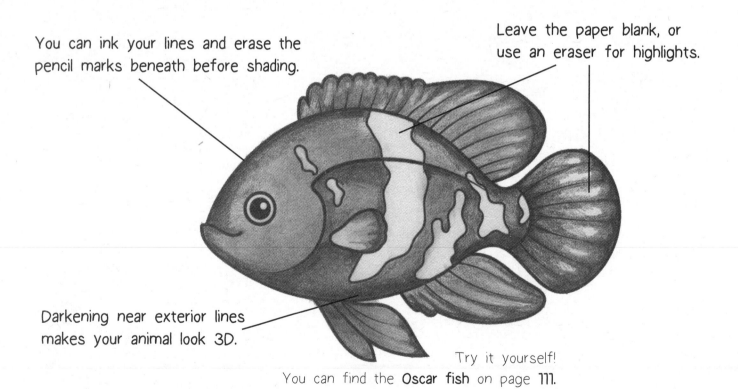

Darkening near exterior lines makes your animal look 3D.

Try it yourself!
You can find the **Oscar fish** on page 111.

MoSt imPortantly: Have FuN!

Domestic Mammals

Beagle

Chihuahua

Corgi

 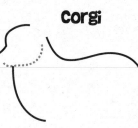 

Pug

German Shepherd

Bassett Hound

Irish Setter

Husky

Bernese Mountain Dog

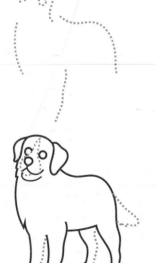
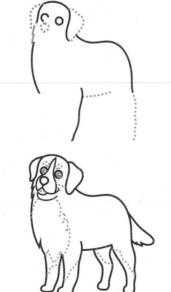
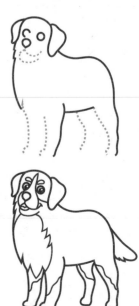

Coonhound

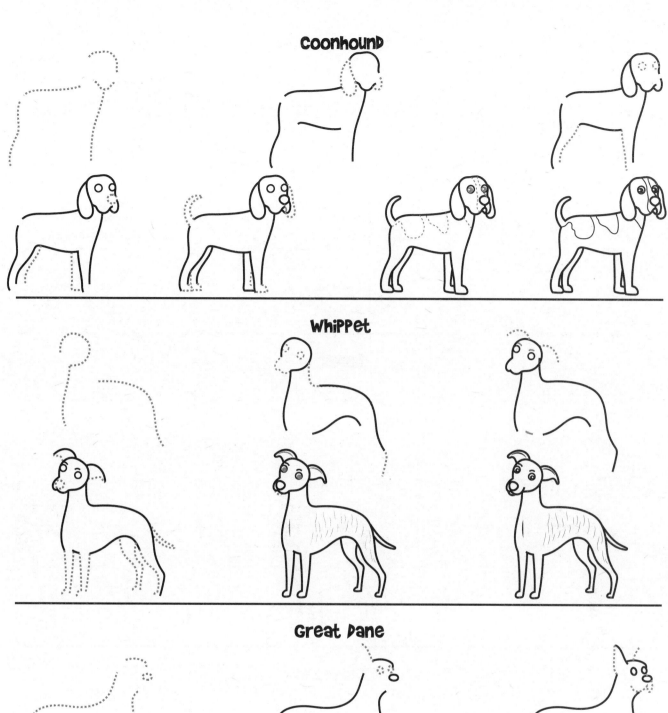

Whippet

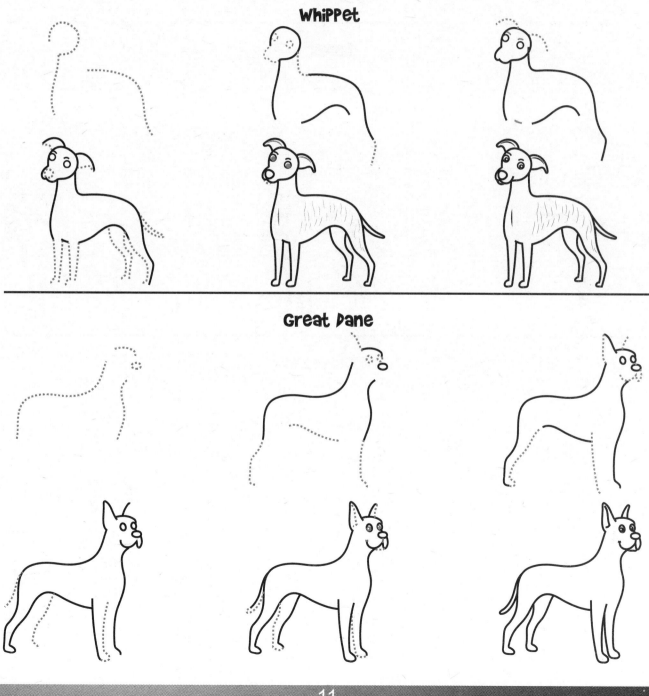

Great Dane

Golden Retriever

Boxer
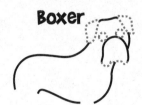

Dobermann
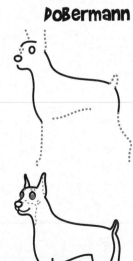
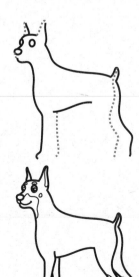

12

LaBrador Retriever

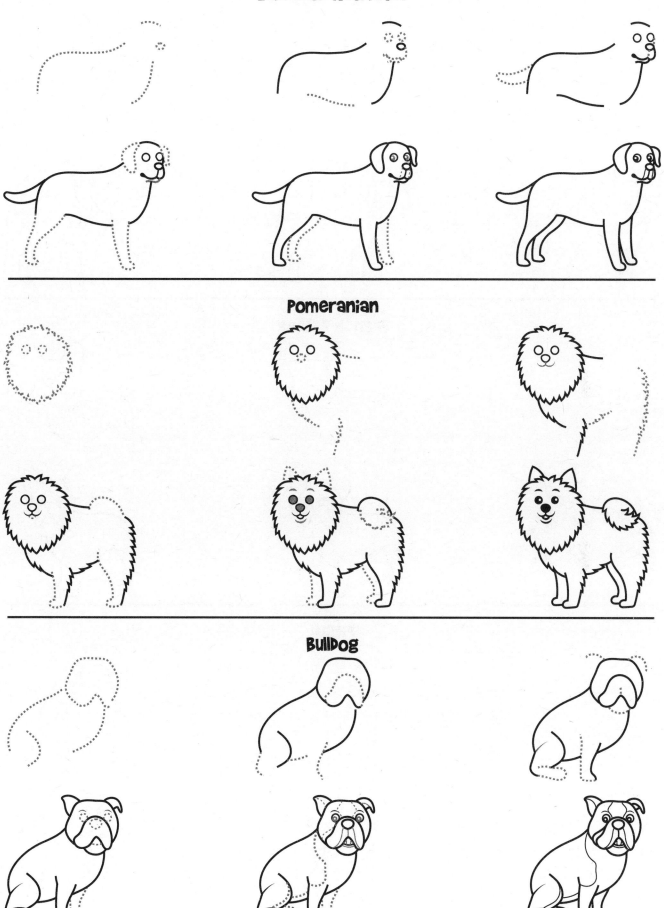

Pomeranian

BullDog

Akita

French Bulldog

PitBull

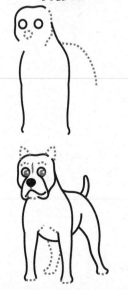
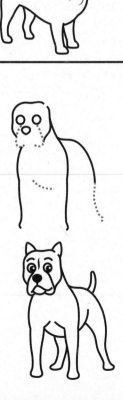

Pug Puppy

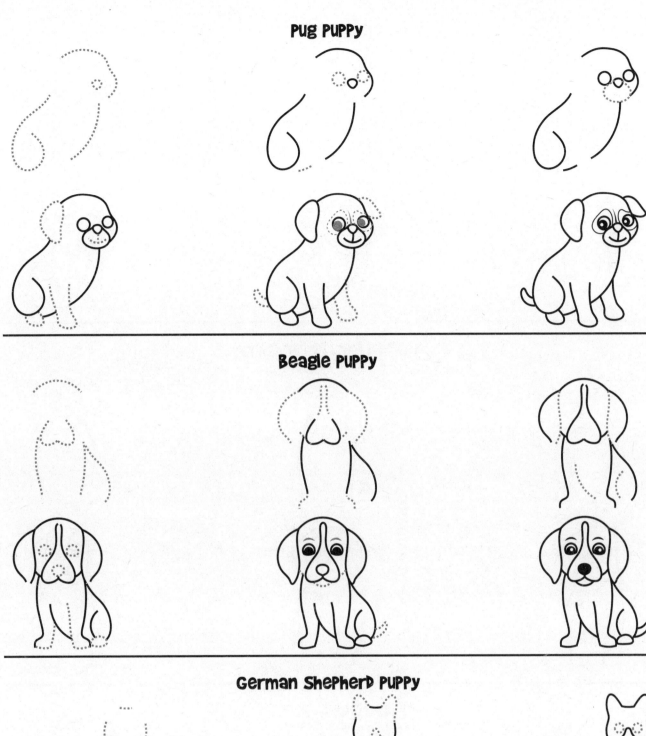

Beagle Puppy

German Shepherd Puppy

Corgi PUPPY

Golden Retriever PUPPY

Chihuahua PUPPY

Siamese cat

American Shorthair Cat

Russian Blue cat

Longhair cat

Munchkin cat

Bengal cat

Maine Coon Cat

Sphynx Hairless Cat

Ragdoll Cat

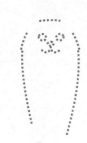  

Siamese Kitten

American Shorthair Kitten

Ragdoll Kitten

Munchkin Kitten

Sphynx Hairless Kitten

Arabian Horse

Norwegian Fjord Horse

Akhal-Teke Horse

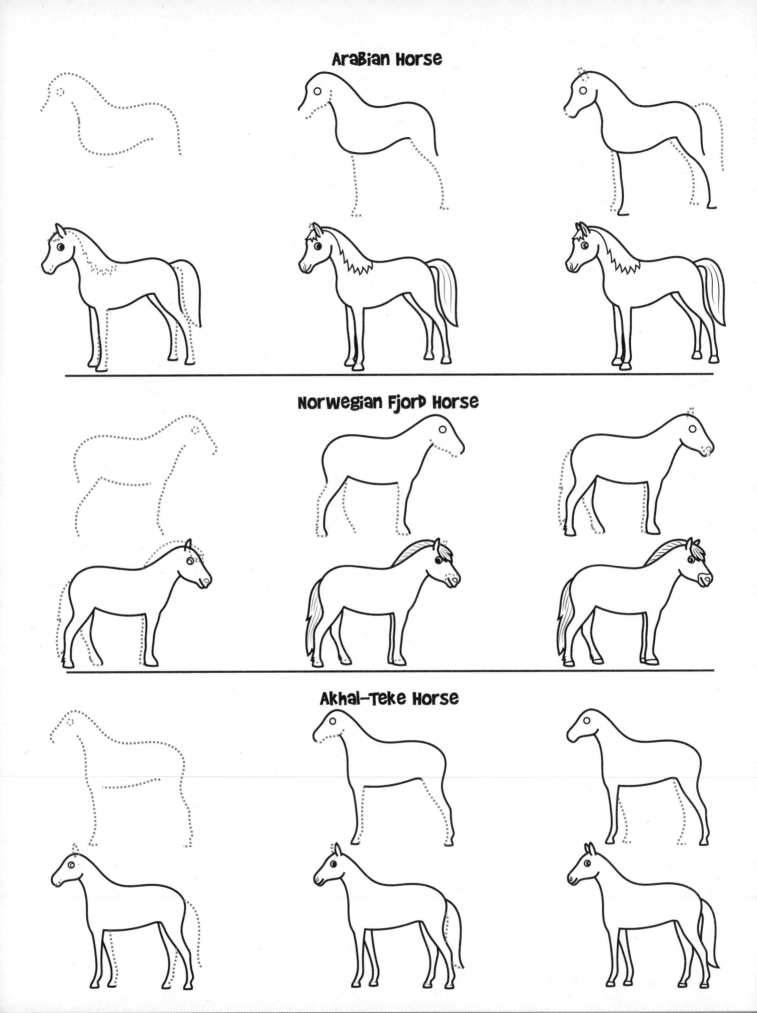

Mustang Horse

Friesian Horse

Clydesdale Horse

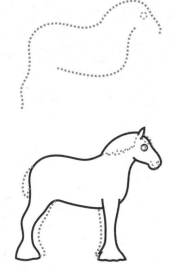
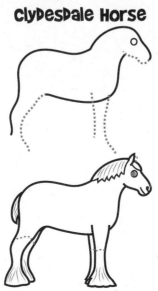

Shetland Pony

 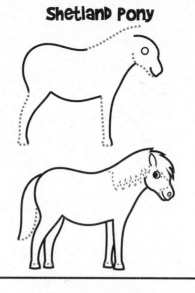 

Dales Pony

 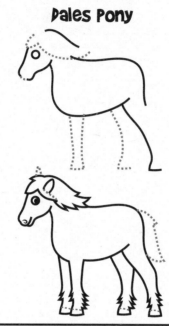 

American Miniature Pony

Sheep

Domestic Goat

Donkey

yak

 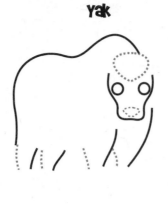 

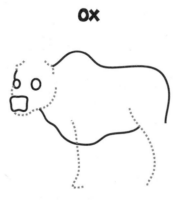 

---

ox

Water Buffalo

Cow

Pig

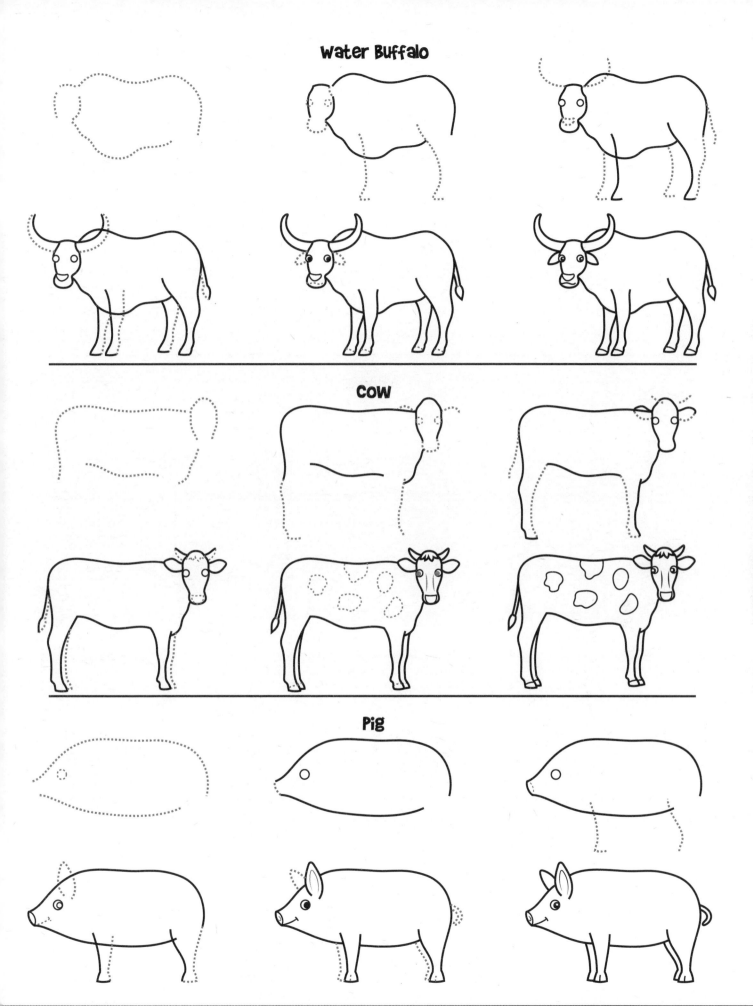

Vietnamese PotBelly Pig

Alpaca

Rabbit

Hamster

Chinchilla

Gerbil

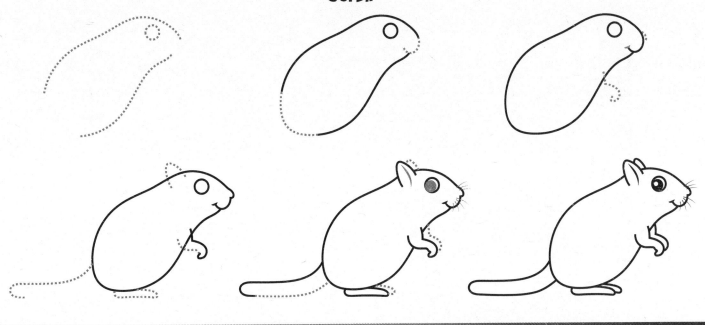

Need some space to practice?
Give it a shot here!

WilD Mammals

Lynx

Tiger

Snow Leopard

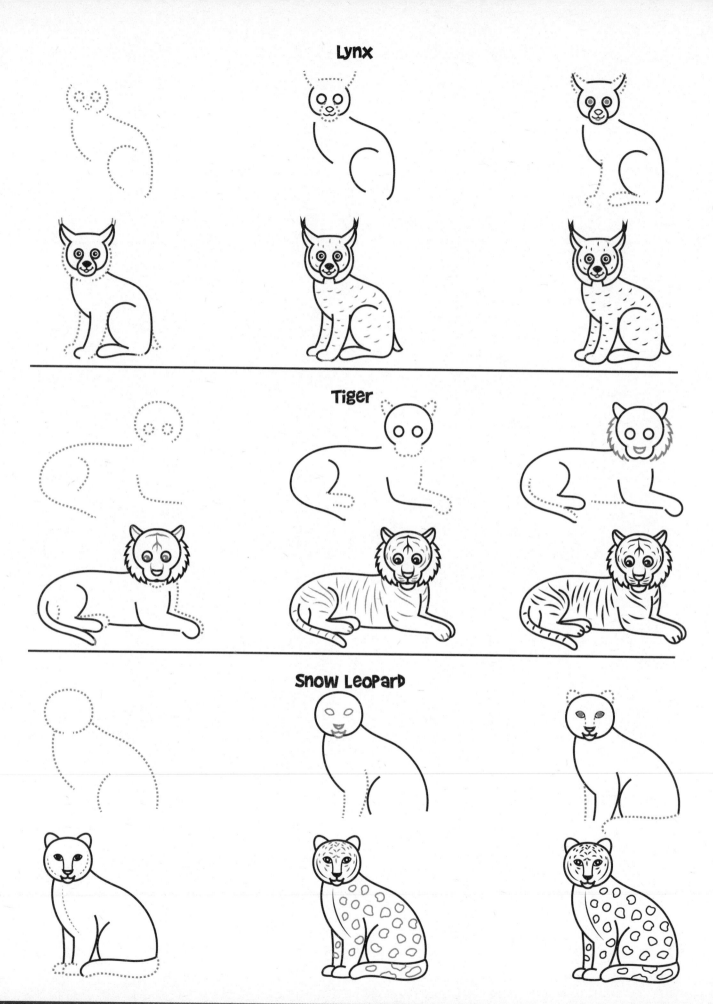

32

cougar

ocelot

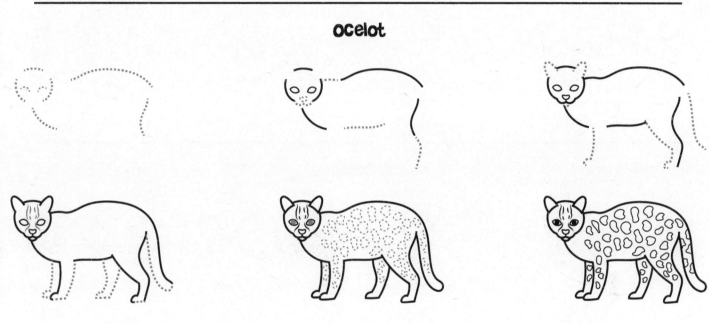

caracal

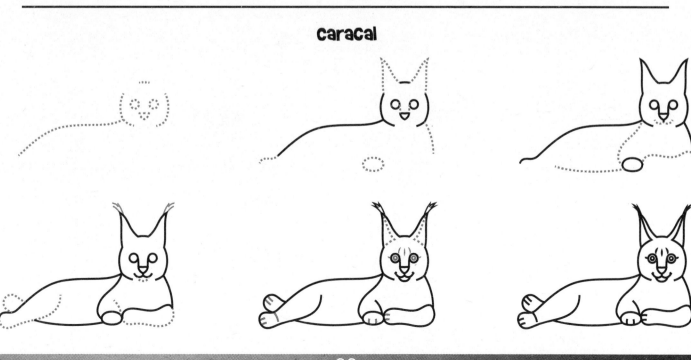

Jaguar

Cheetah

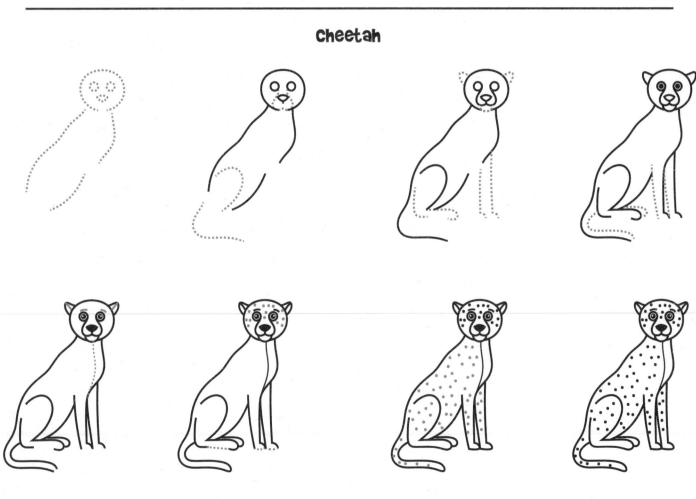

Female Lion

Lion Cub

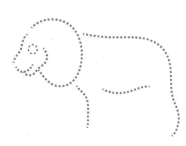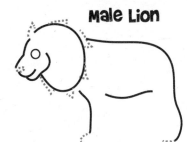

Male Lion

Giraffe

Okapi

Dromedary Camel

 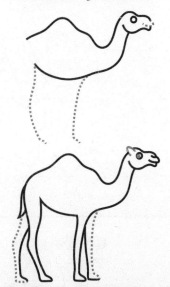 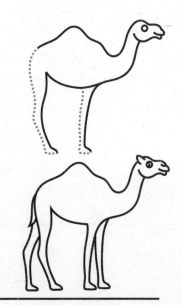

Bactrian Camel

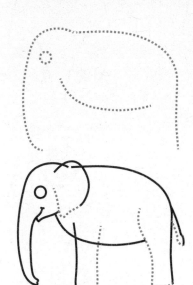 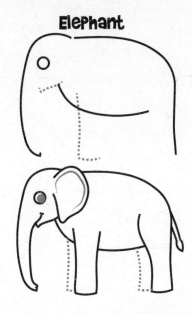 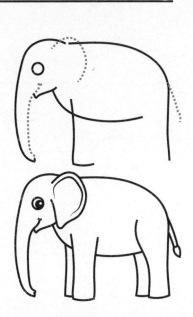

Elephant

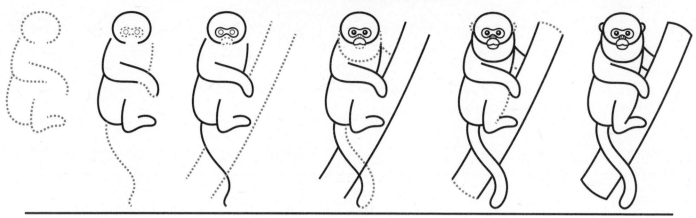

Golden snub-nosed monkey

Gorilla

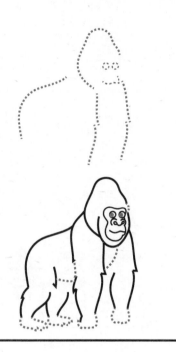
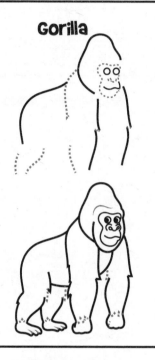
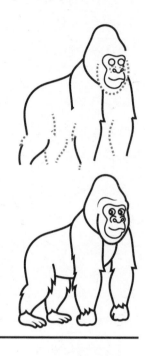

Chimpanzee

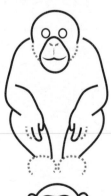

Lemur

Orangutan

Guinea Baboon

Mandrill

Gibbon

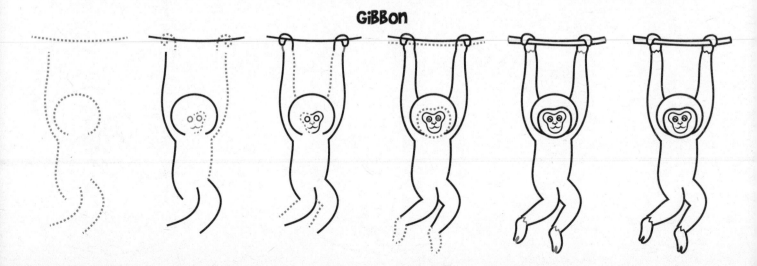

Tamarin

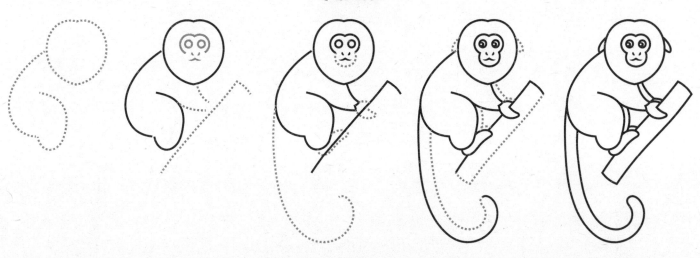

Capuchin

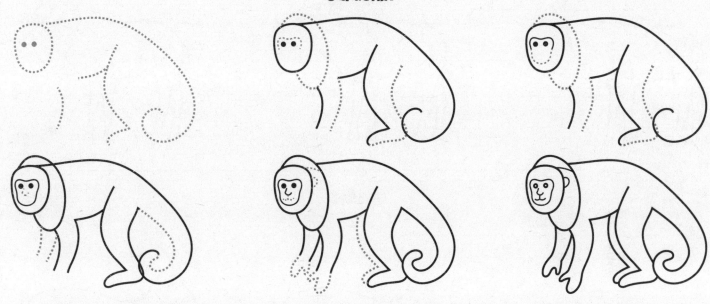

Marmoset

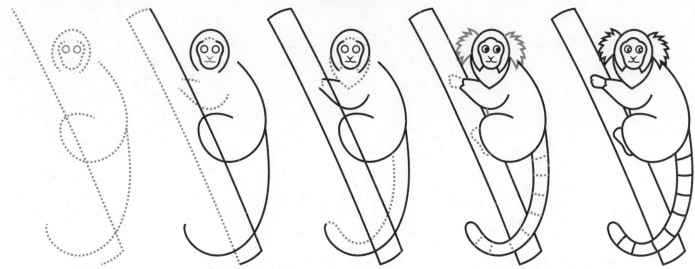

Stag

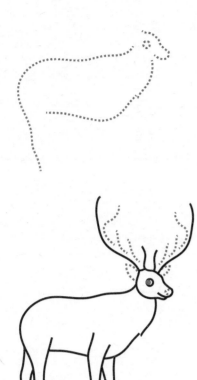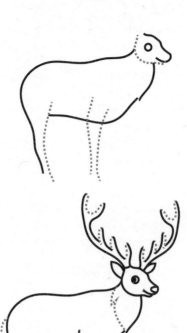

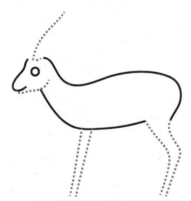

Gazelle

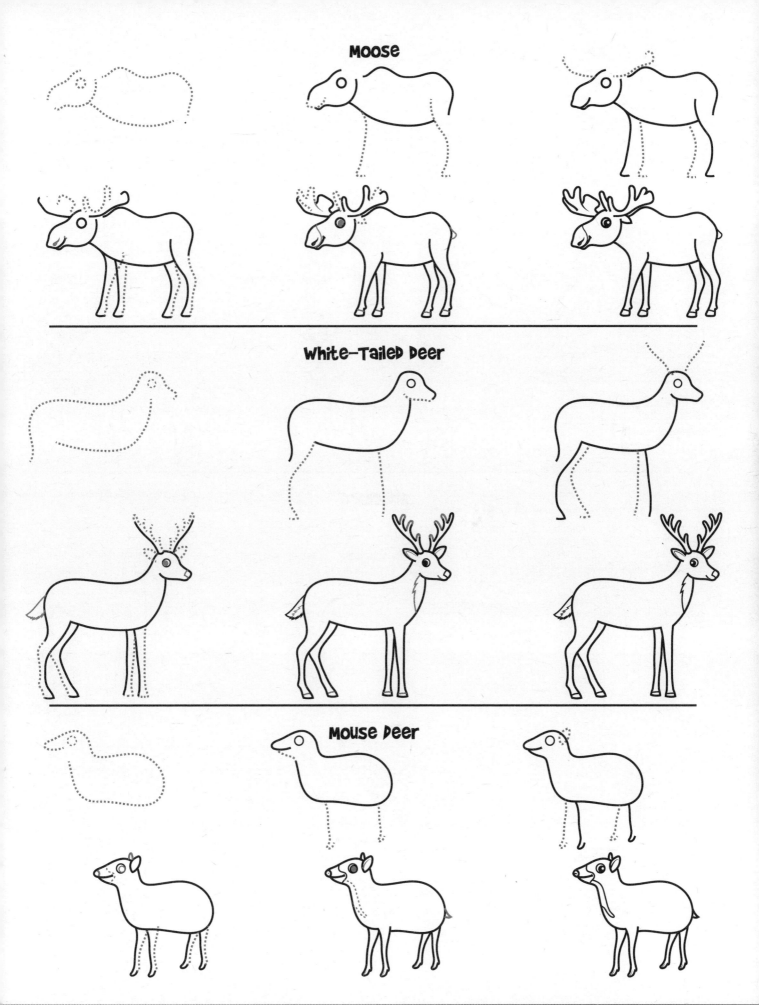

MOOSE

WHITE-TAILED DEER

MOUSE DEER

43

Elk

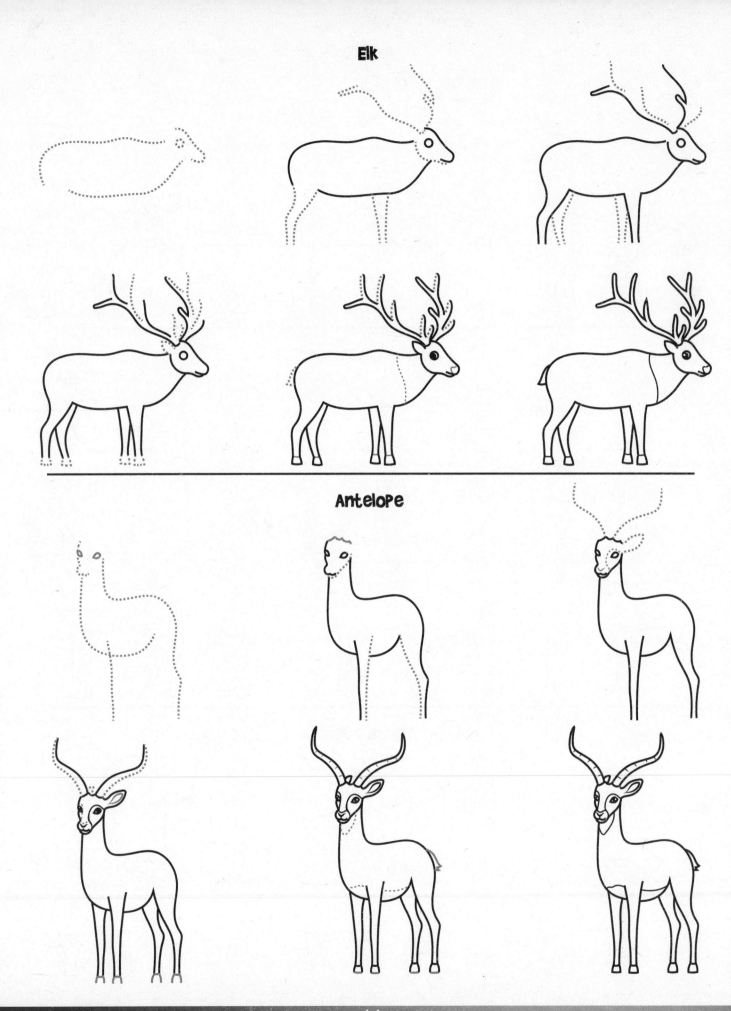

Antelope

Reindeer

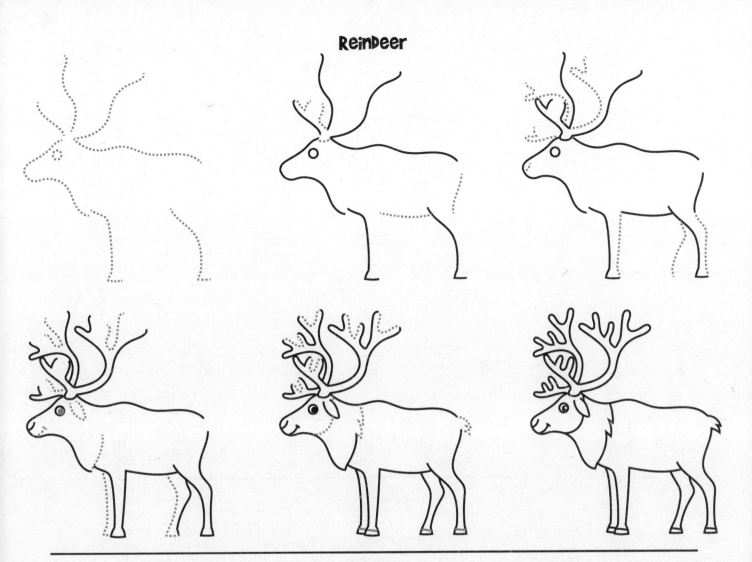

Dik-Dik

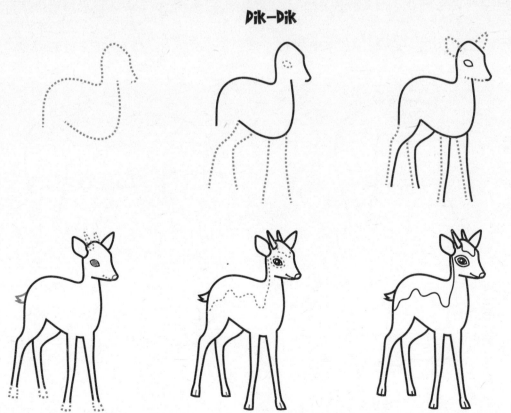

Llama

Black Bear

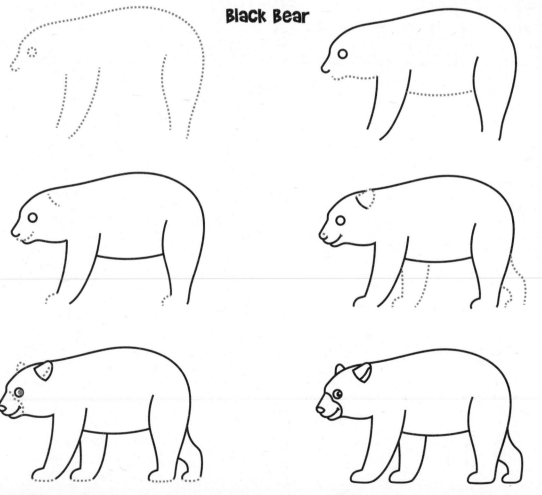

Sloth Bear

Giant Panda

Grizzly Bear

Koala

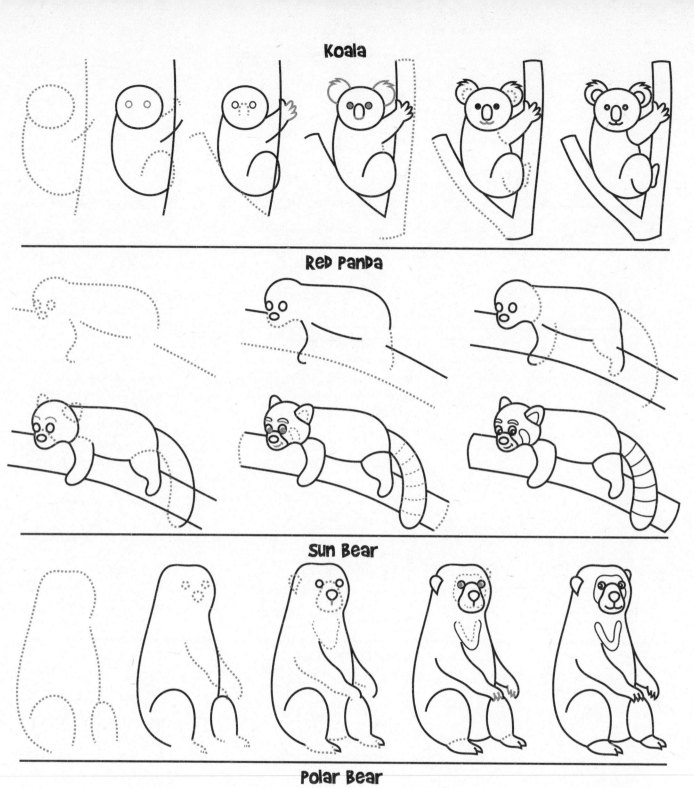

Red Panda

Sun Bear

Polar Bear

Siberian Ibex

Argali Goat

Bighorn Sheep

Rhino

Hippopotamus

cape Buffalo

Takin

WildeBeest

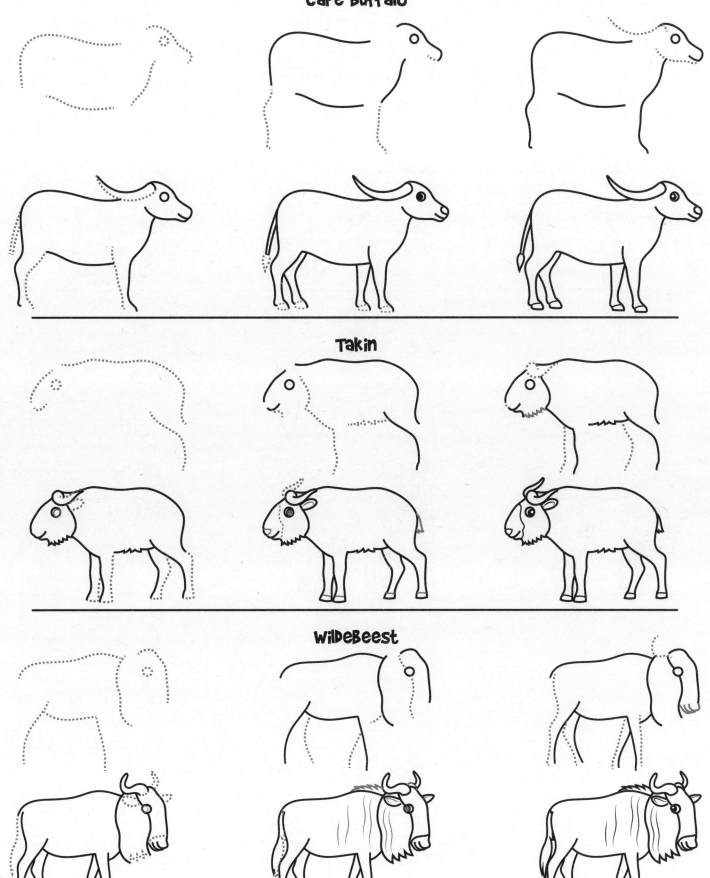

Hyena

Zebra

Tapir

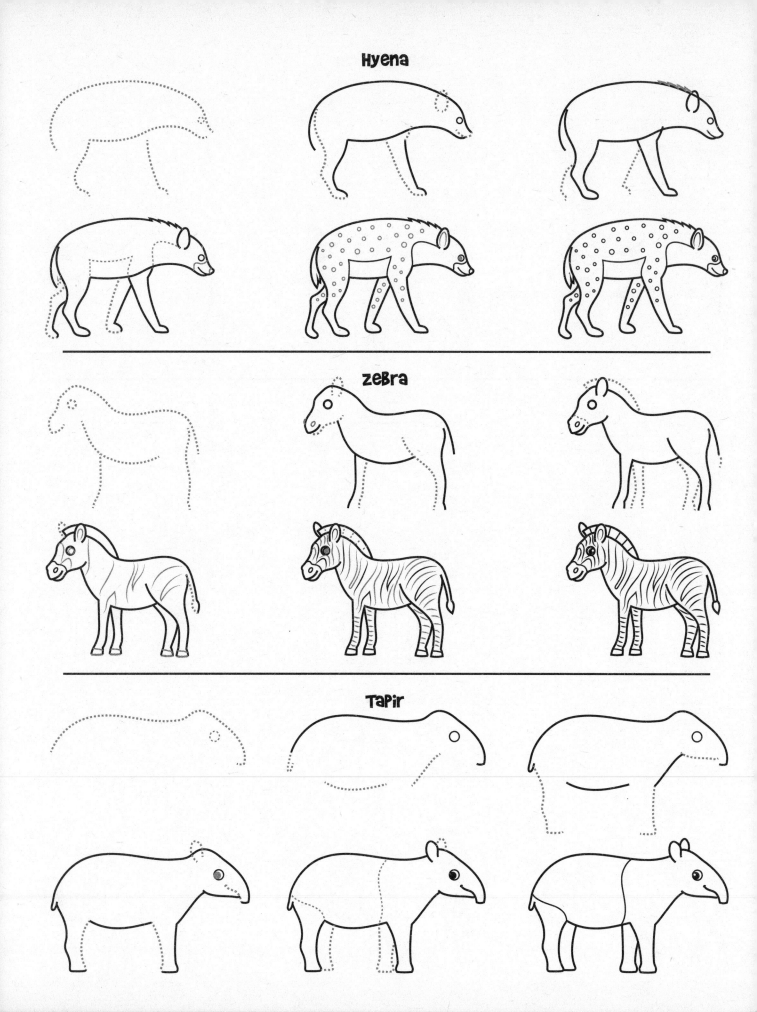

Wild Boar

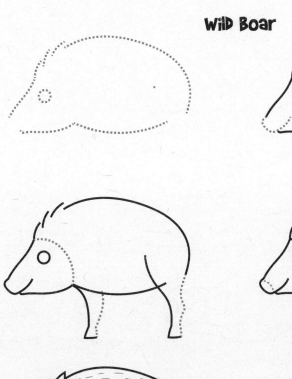

Pangolin

Sloth

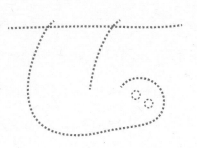
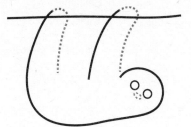
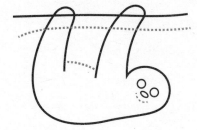

Anteater

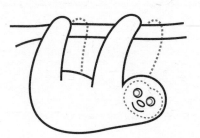
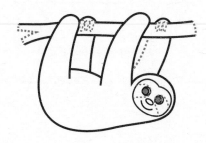

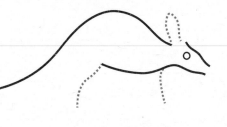

Aardvark

WomBat

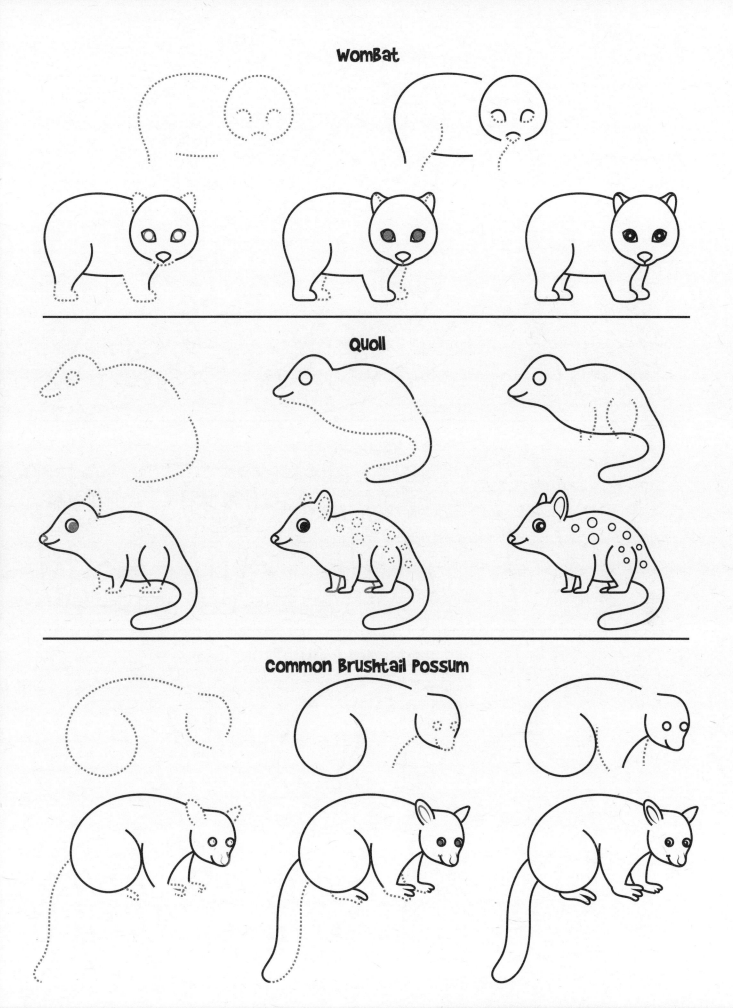

Quoll

Common Brushtail Possum

Tasmanian Devil

Raccoon

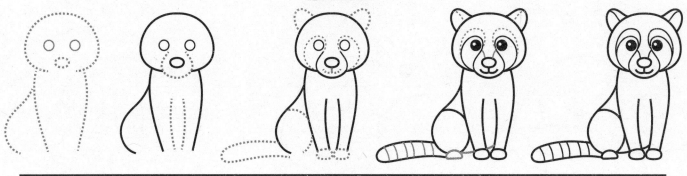

Ring-Tailed Coati

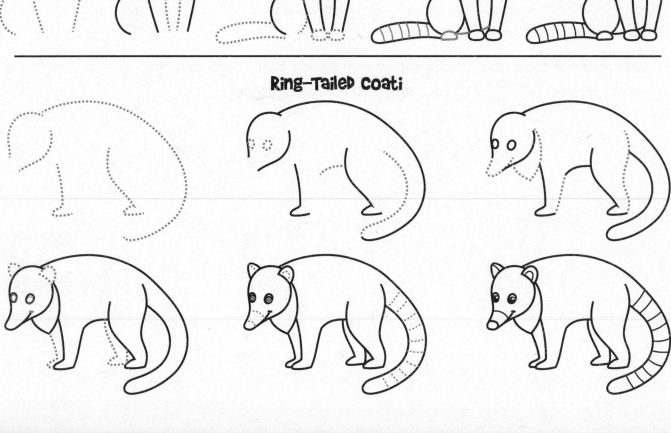

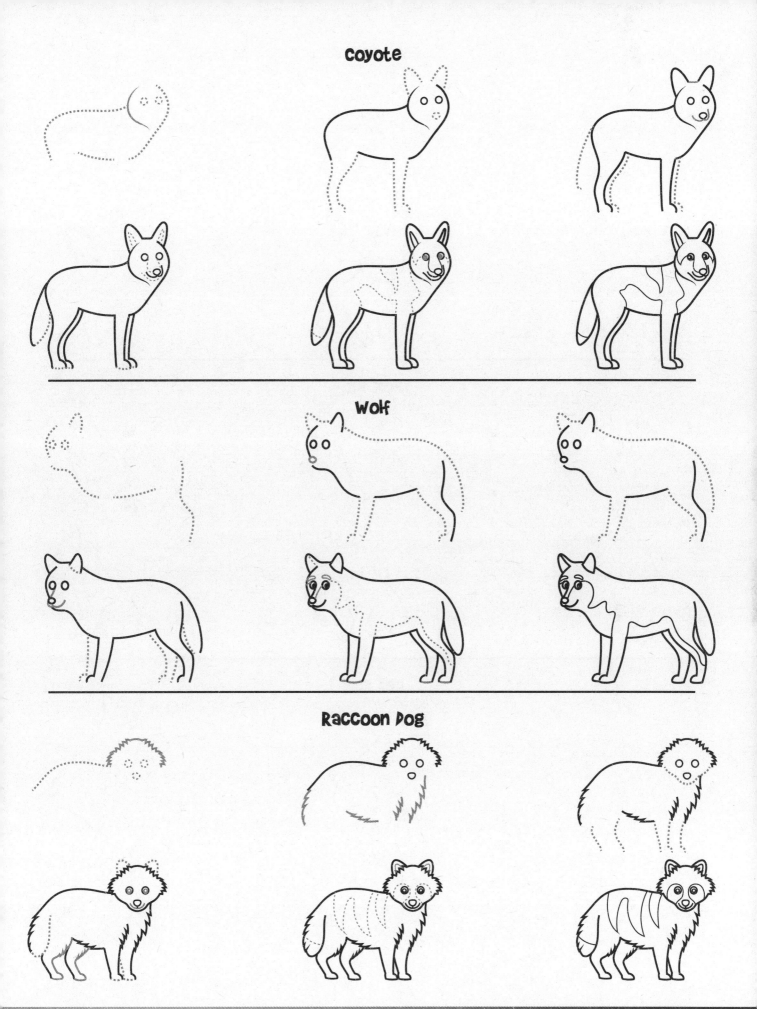

coyote

Wolf

Raccoon Dog

Fennec Fox

Fox Kit

Red Fox

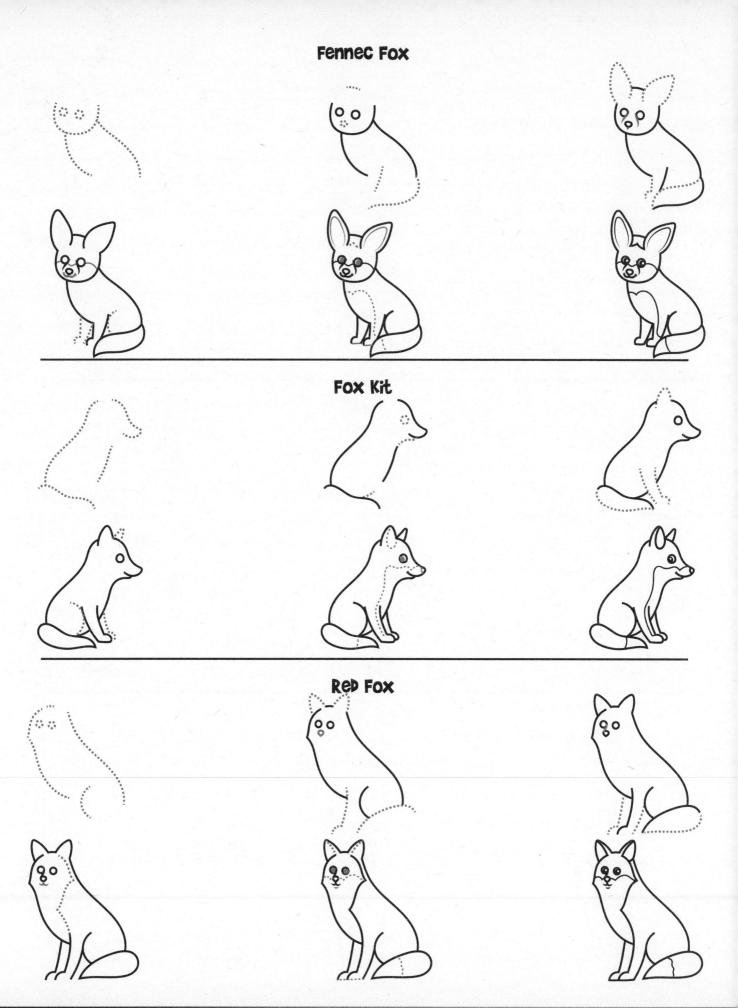

Kangaroo

Quokka

Honey Badger

Hedgehog

Opossum

Bat

Beaver

Platypus

Otter

Armadillo

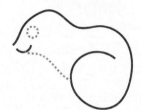

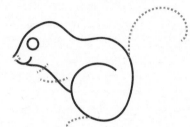

Chipmunk

Groundhog

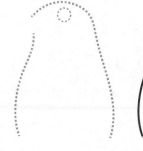

CAPYBara

PorCUPine

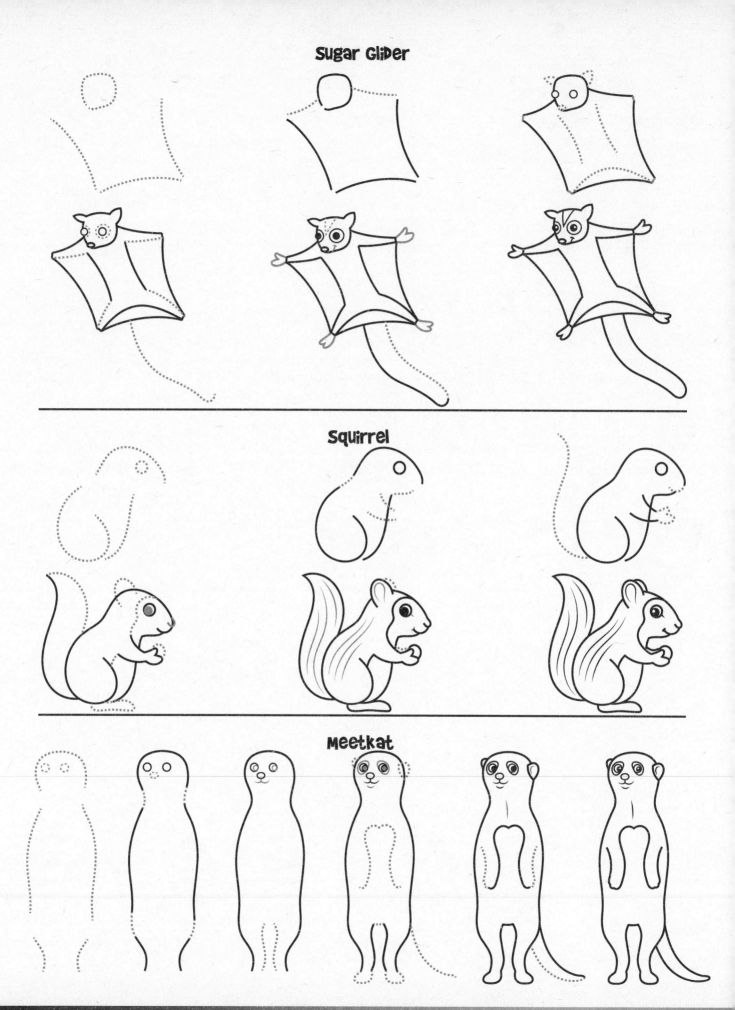

Sugar Glider

Squirrel

Meetkat

Rat

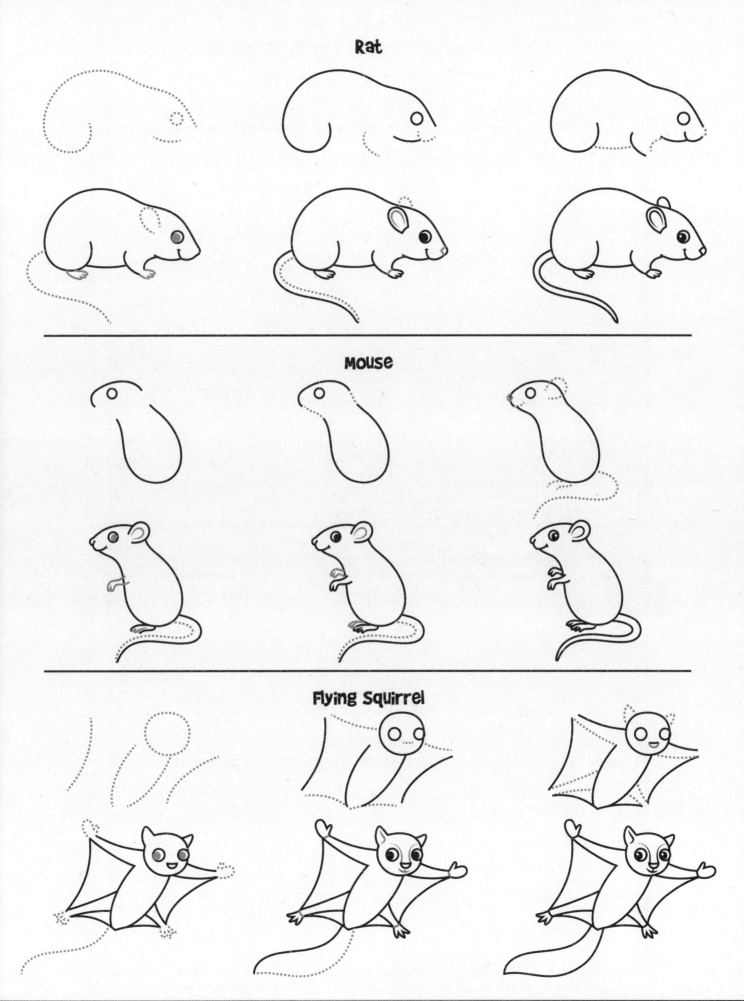

Mouse

Flying Squirrel

NEED some space to Practice?
Give it a shot here!

BirDs

Blue Jay

Budgie

Cardinal

crane

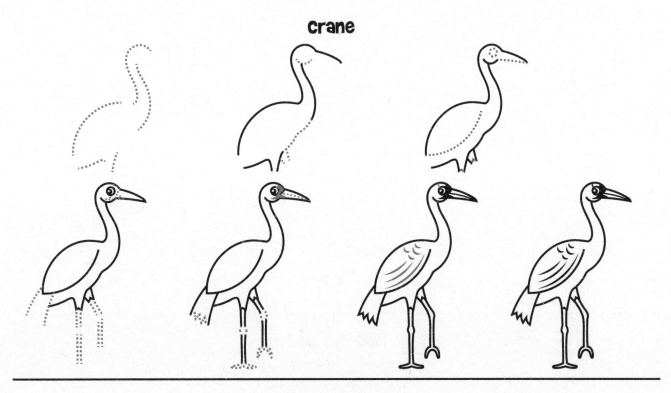

common Kestrel

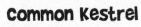

ChiCKen

Duck

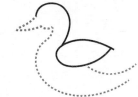

Golden Eagle

Bald Eagle

Barn owl

Long-Crested Eagle

Steller's Sea Eagle

White Hawk

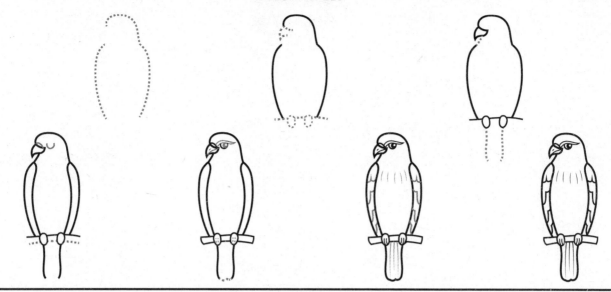

Gyrfalcon

Eurasian Sparrowhawk

Goose

HummingBird

Flamingo

KookaBurra

Great HornBill

Emu

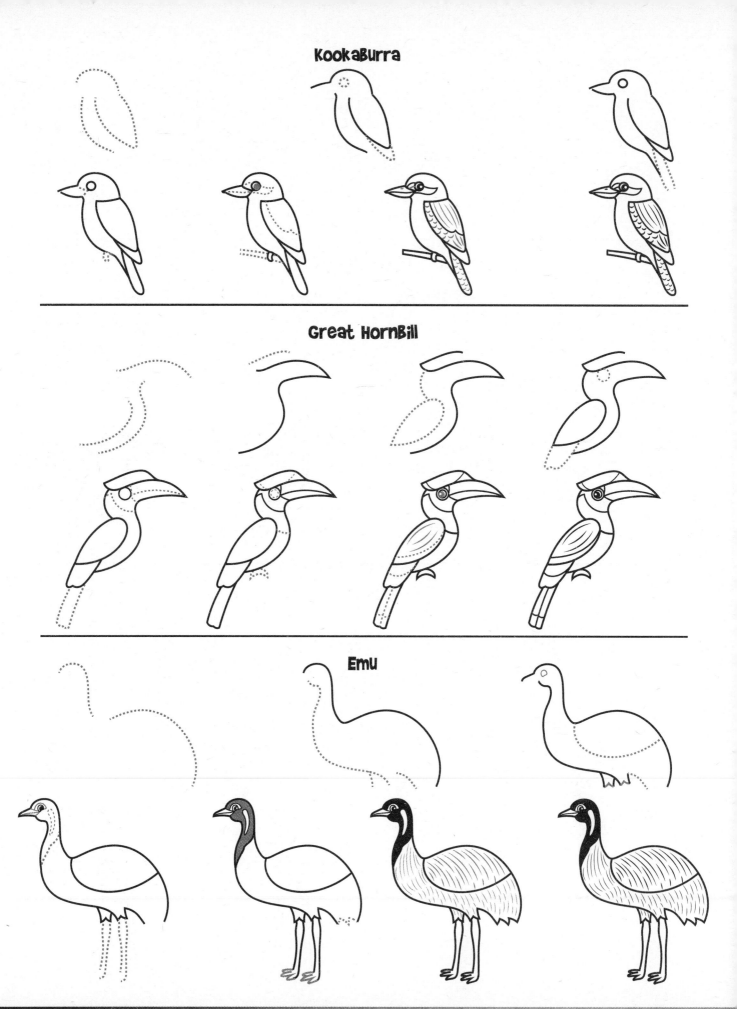

Quail

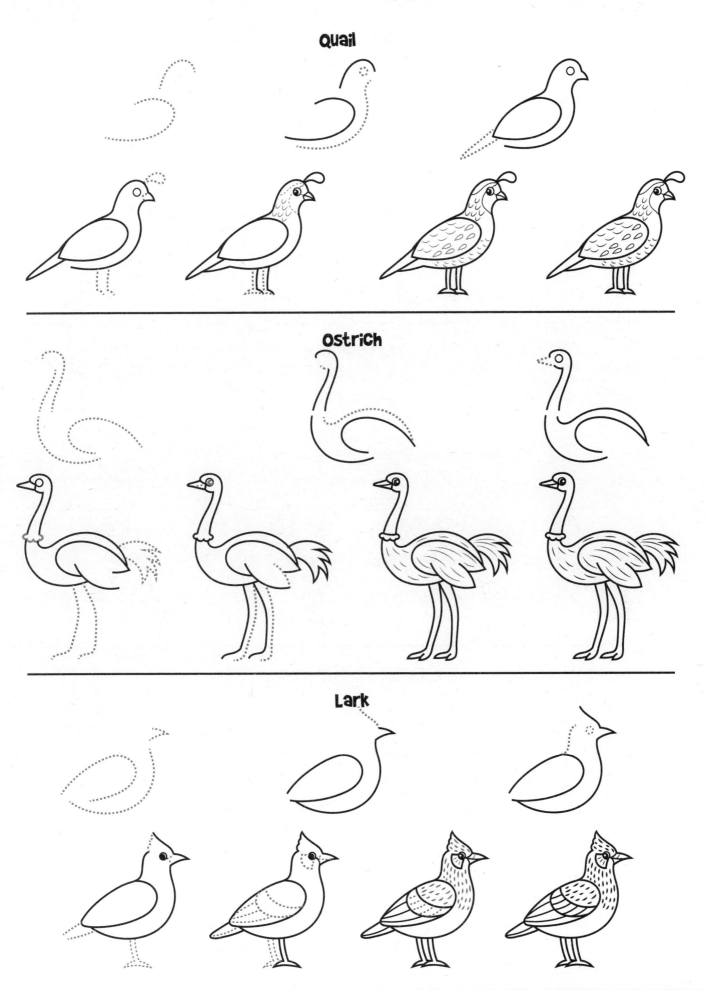

Ostrich

Lark

Snowy Owl

Screech Owl

Great Horned Owl

Scarlet Macaw

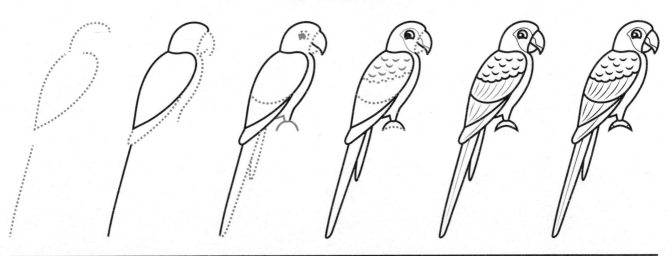

Rose-Breasted Cockatoo

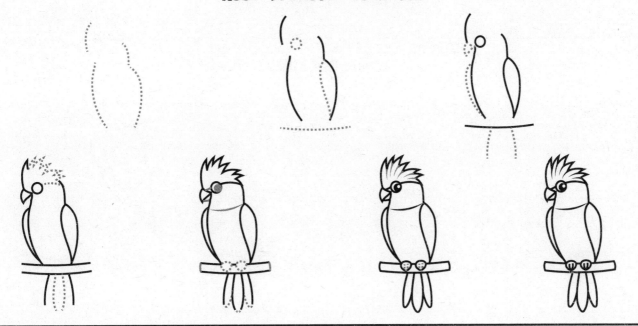

Blue Crown Conure

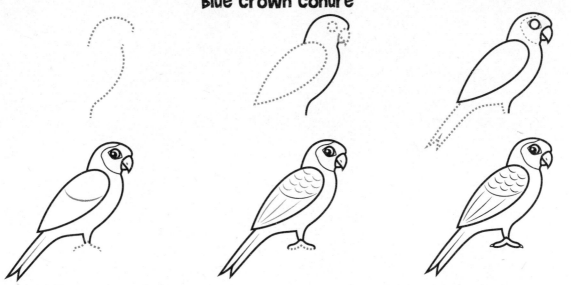

Pelican

White Cockatoo

Penguin

Rooster

RoaDrunner

Raven

Swan

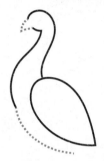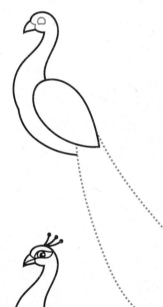

Peacock

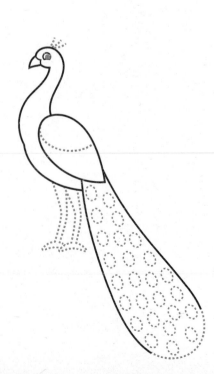

Toucan

Seagull

Turkey

NEED SOME SPACE TO PRACTICE?
Give it a shot here!

Insects & Arachnids

Ant

Ant Queen

Dung Beetle

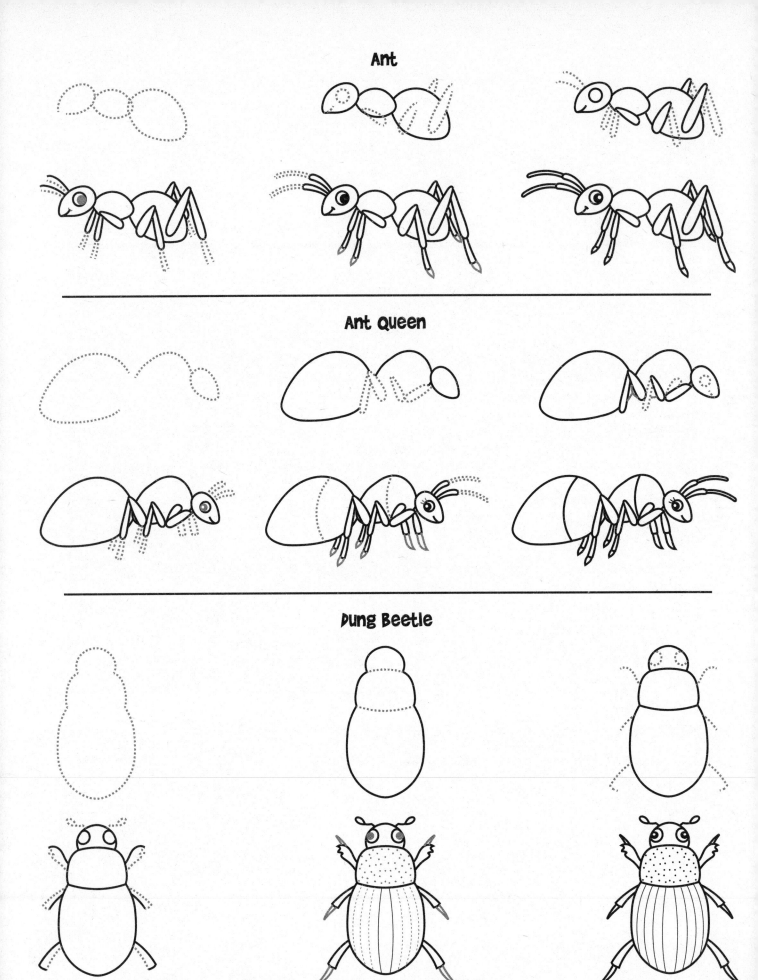

Dragonfly

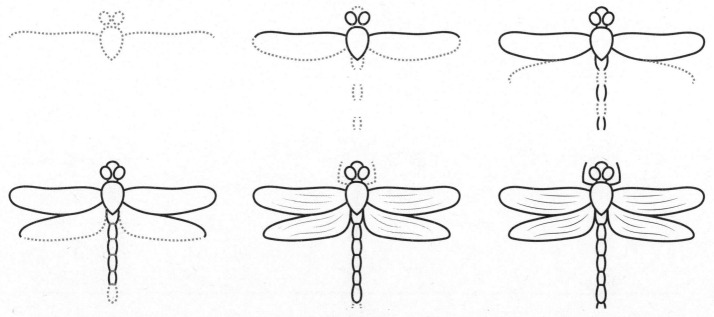

Firefly

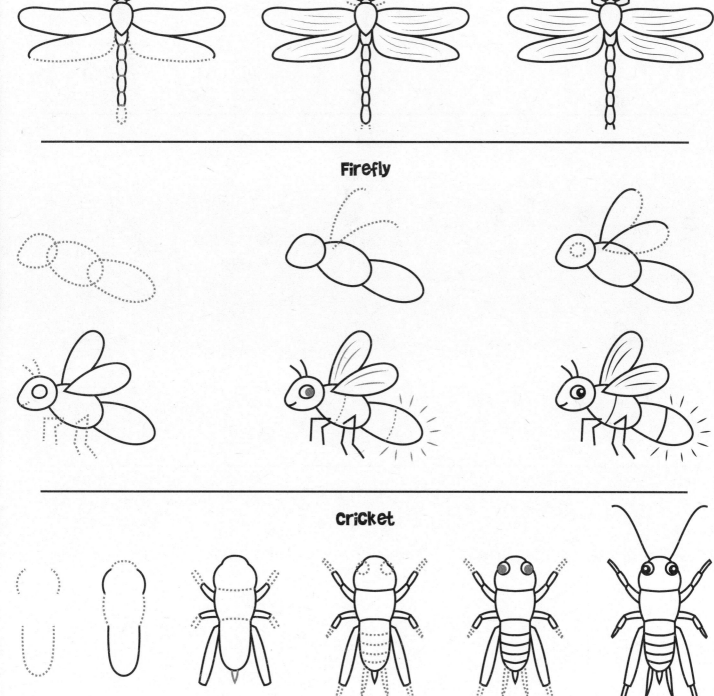

Cricket

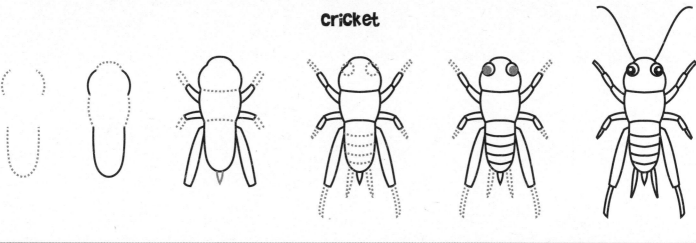

LaDybug

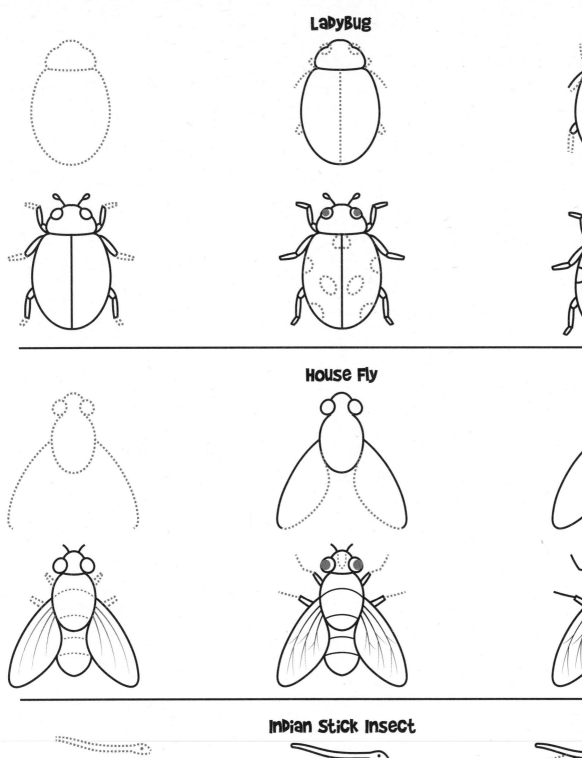

House Fly

InDian Stick Insect

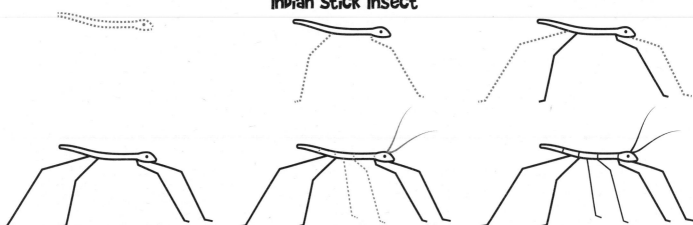

Monarch Caterpillar

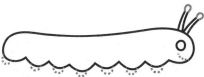  

Monarch Butterfly

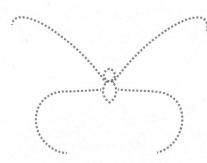 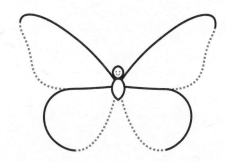 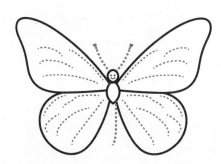

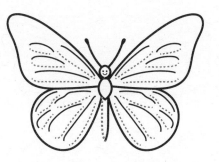  

Rhinoceros Beetle

  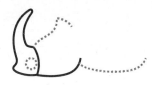 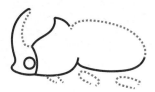

Papilio Ulysses Caterpillar

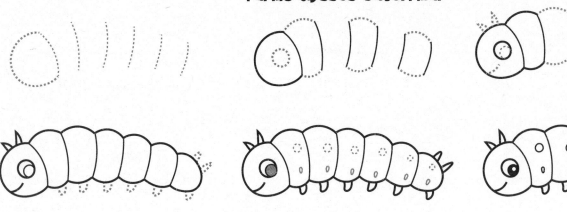

Papilio Ulysses Butterfly

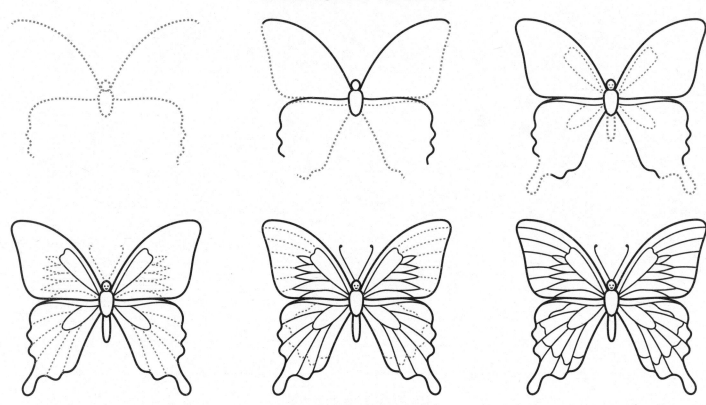

Stag Beetle

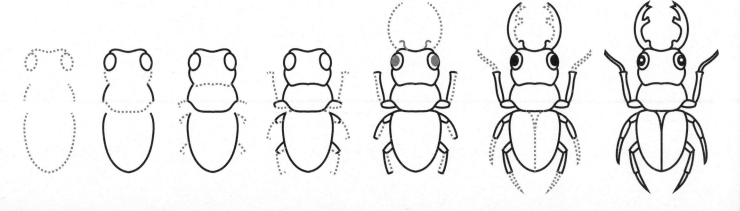

Hornet

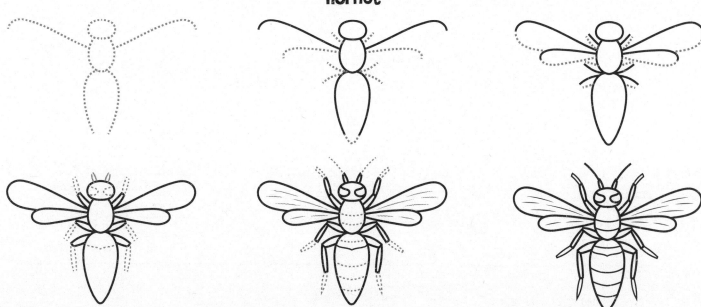

Bumble Bee

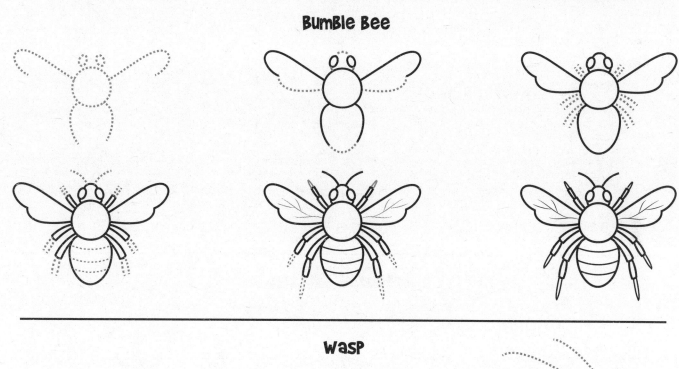

Wasp

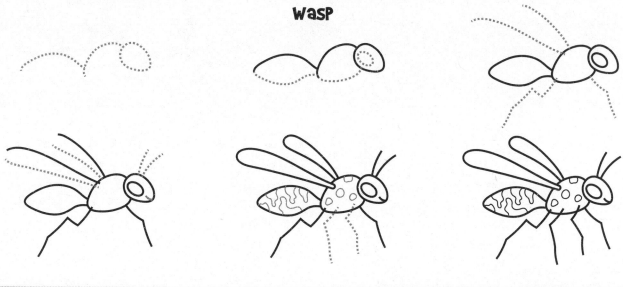

Moth

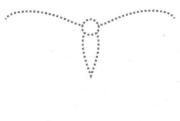

Luna Moth

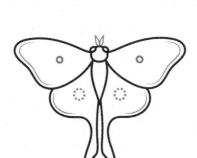

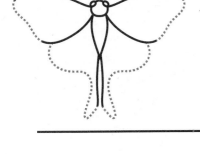
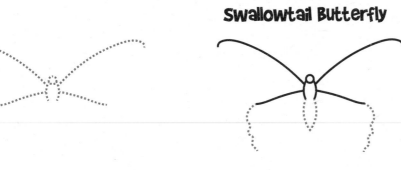

Swallowtail Butterfly

90

Spider

Scorpion

Praying Mantis

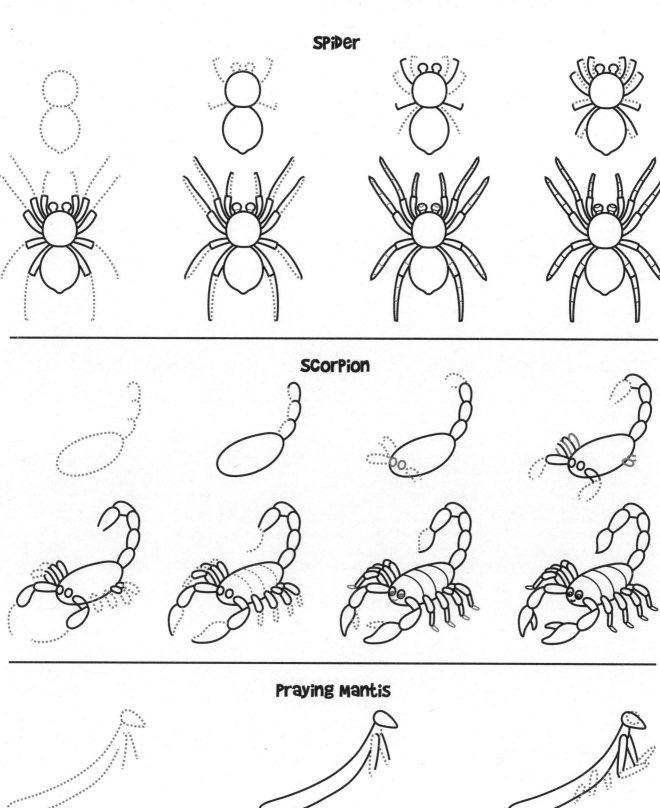

NEED some space to Practice?
Give it a shot here!

Amphibians & Reptiles

Axolotl

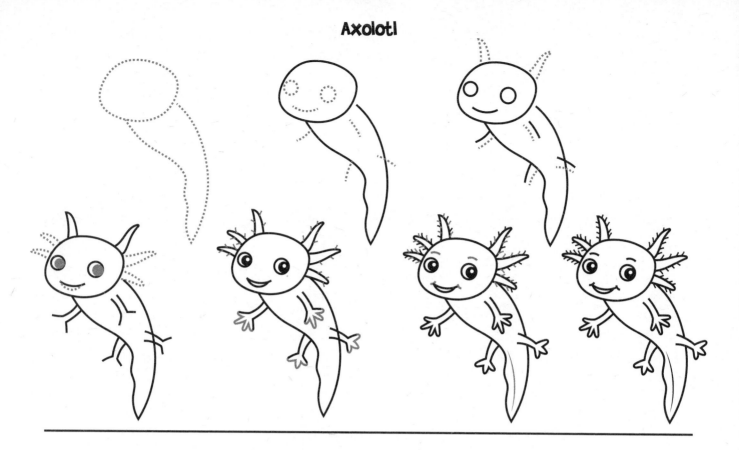

Chinese Giant Salamander

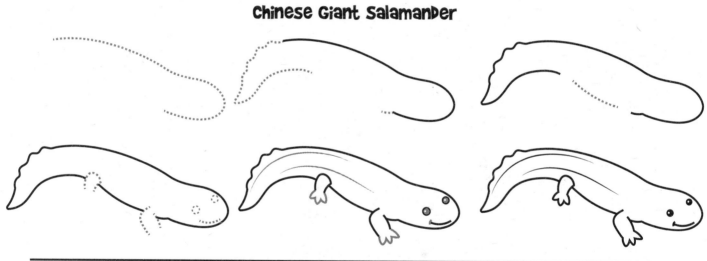

Danube Crested Newt

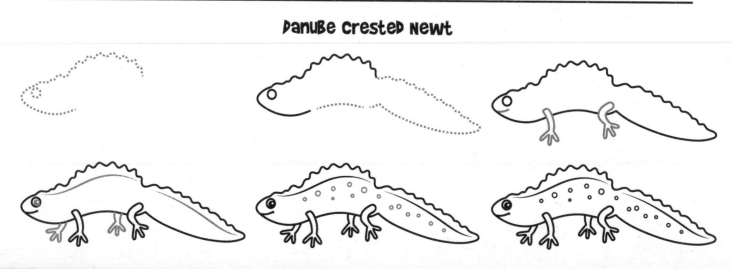

Common Toad

Eastern Newt

Frog Tadpole

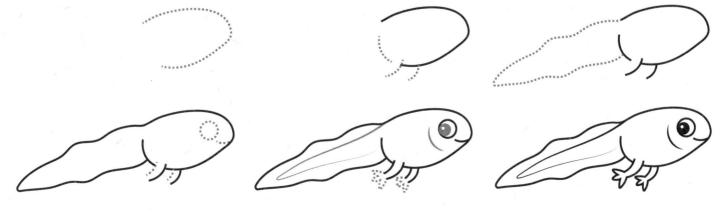

Northern LeoparD Frog

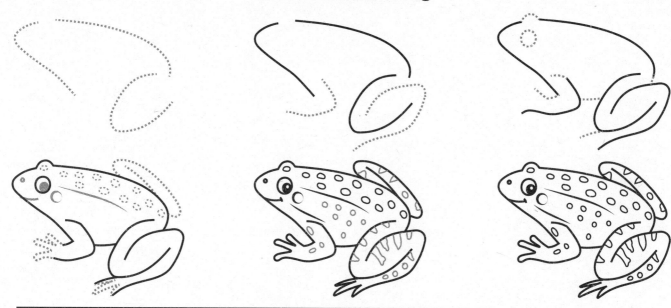

Fire Salamander

Common ReeD Frog

Leaf Frog

Panamanian Golden Frog

Vietnamese Mossy Frog

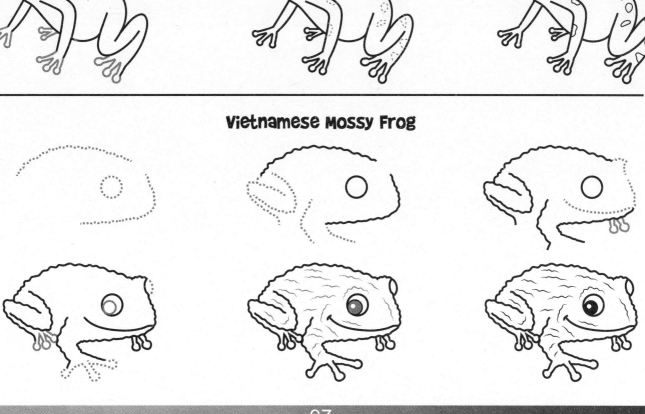

Chrysopelea

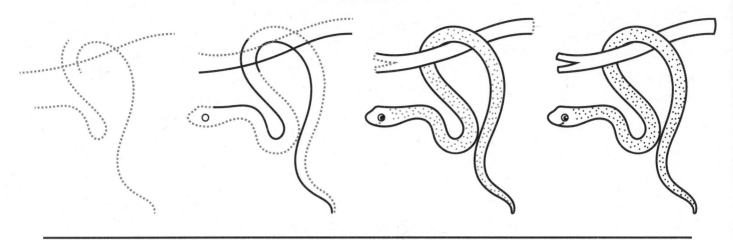

Anaconda

Thorny Devil

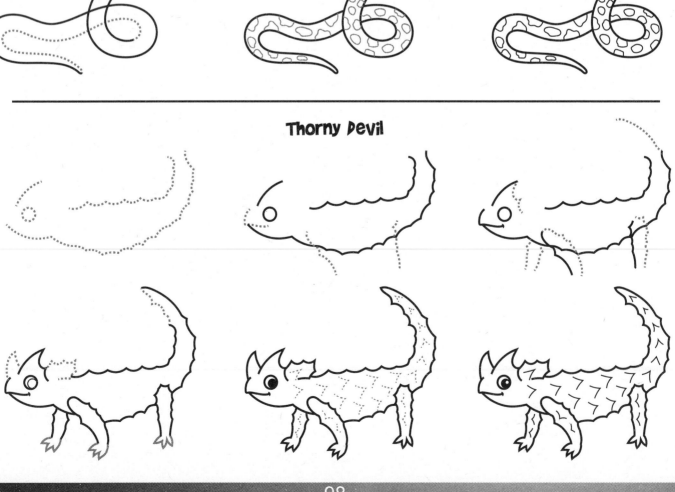

Kingsnake

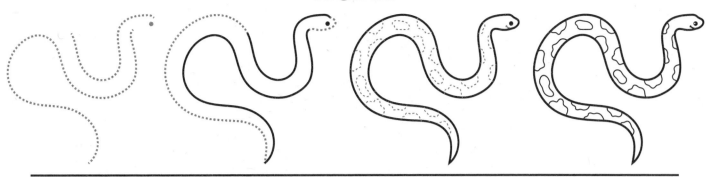

Cobra

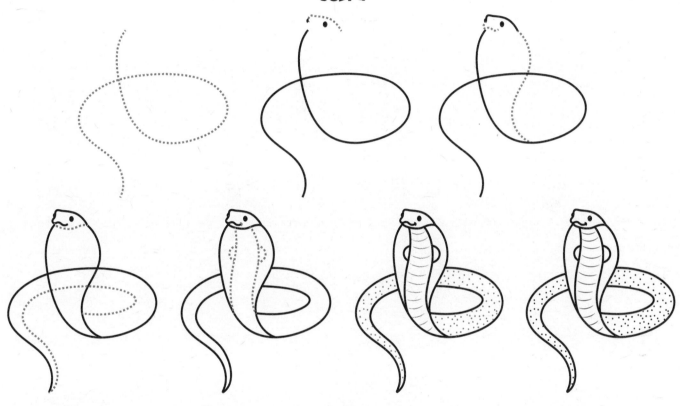

Python

Rattlesnake

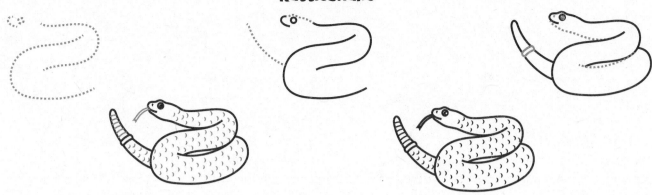

Viperidae

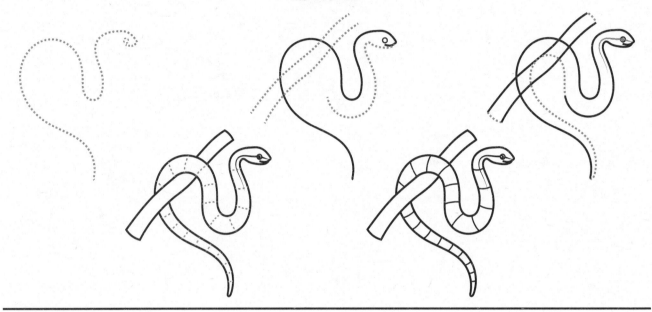

Ahaetulla

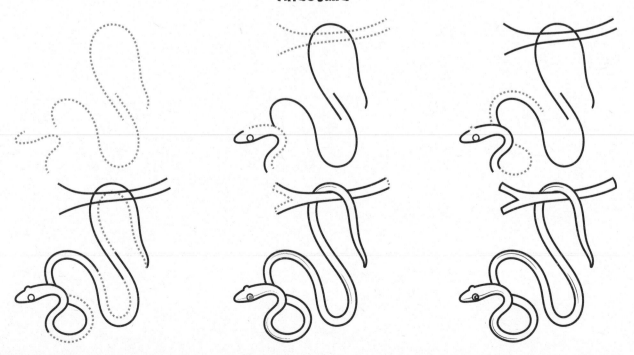

Komodo Dragon

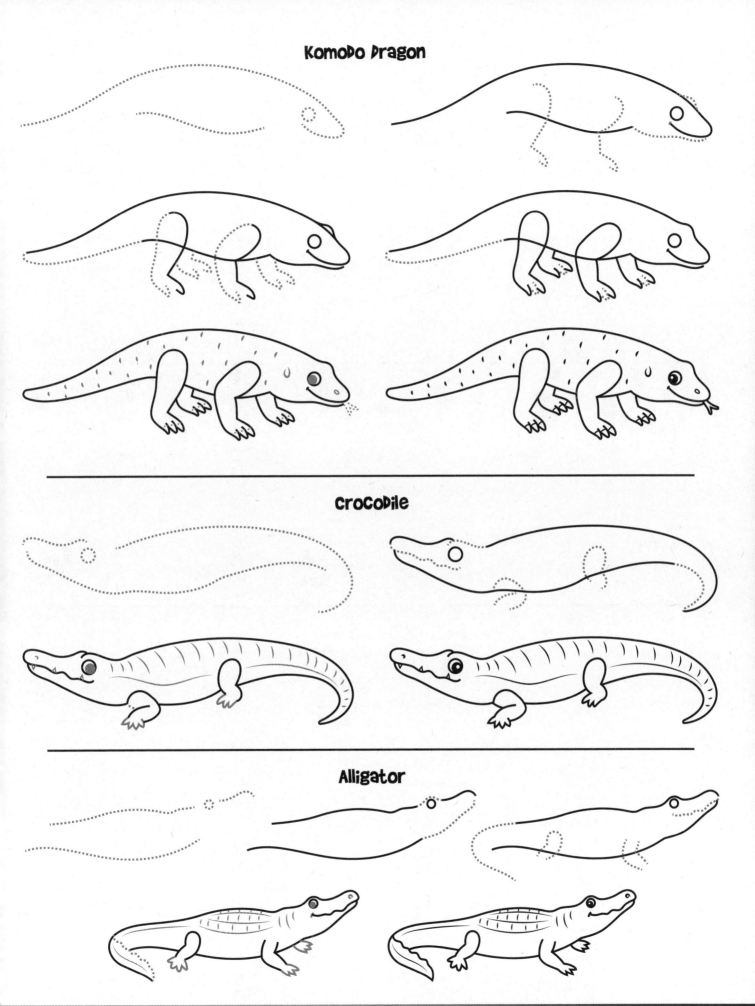

Crocodile

Alligator

Iguana

Leopard Gecko

Gliding Lizard

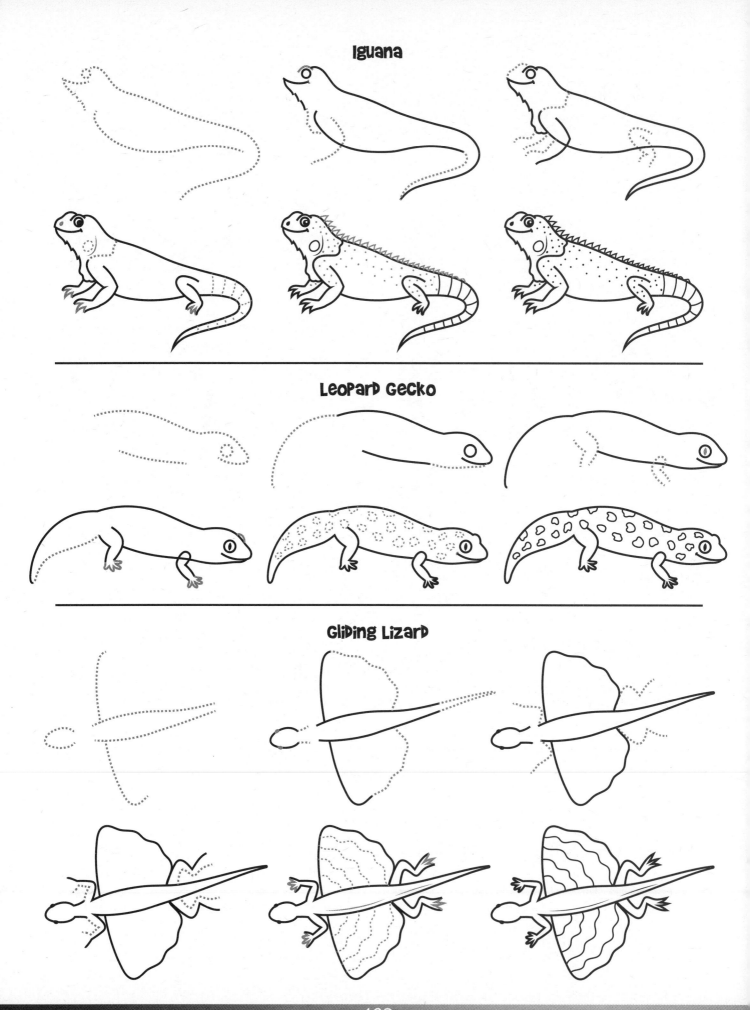

Skink

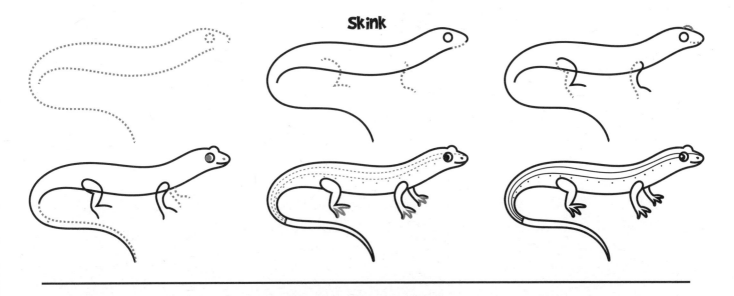

Chinese Water Dragon

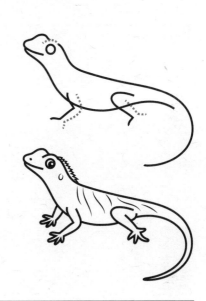

Rock Monitor

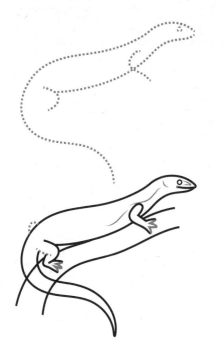
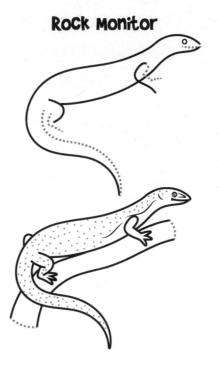
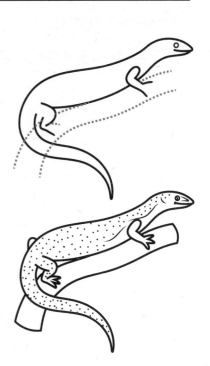

Desert Tortoise

 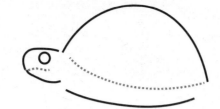 

 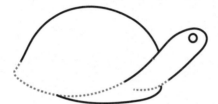 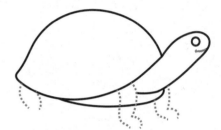

Turtle

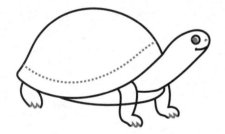  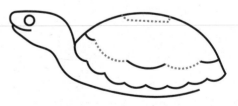

Box Turtle

 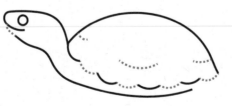 

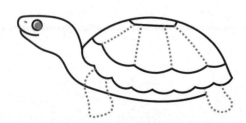  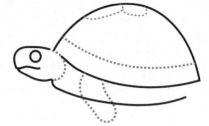

CResTeD GeCKo

BeaRDeD DRagon

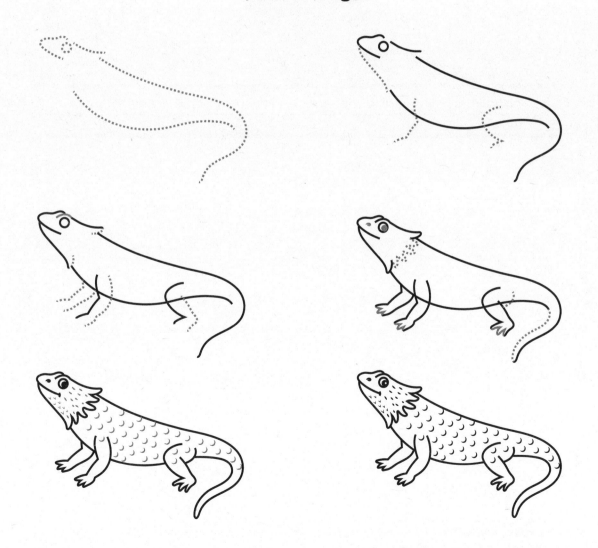

NEED some space to Practice?
Give it a shot here!

Aquatic Animals

Eel

COD

Clownfish

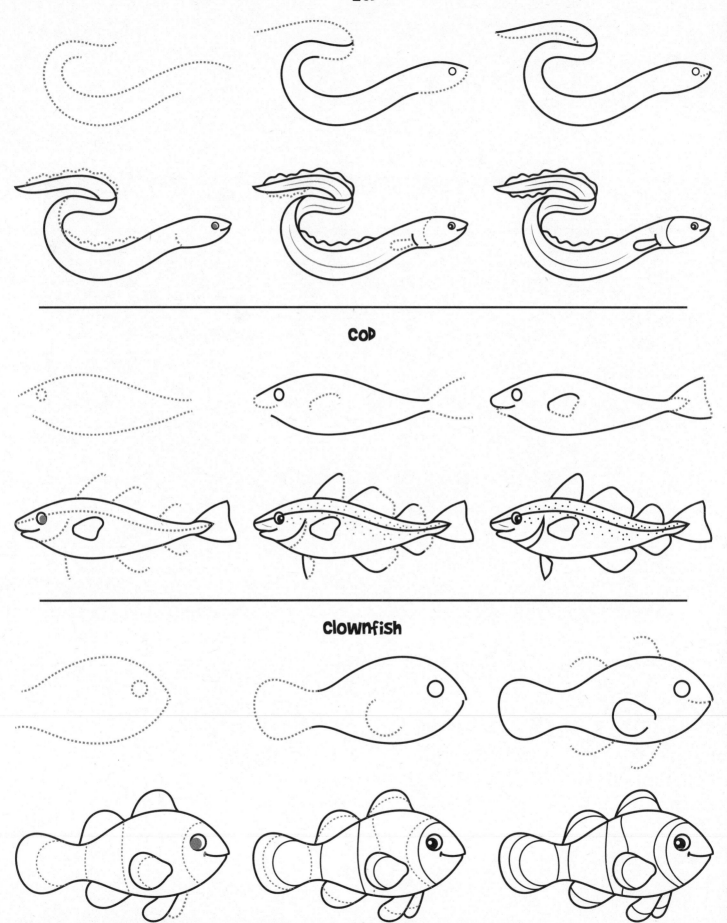

CraB

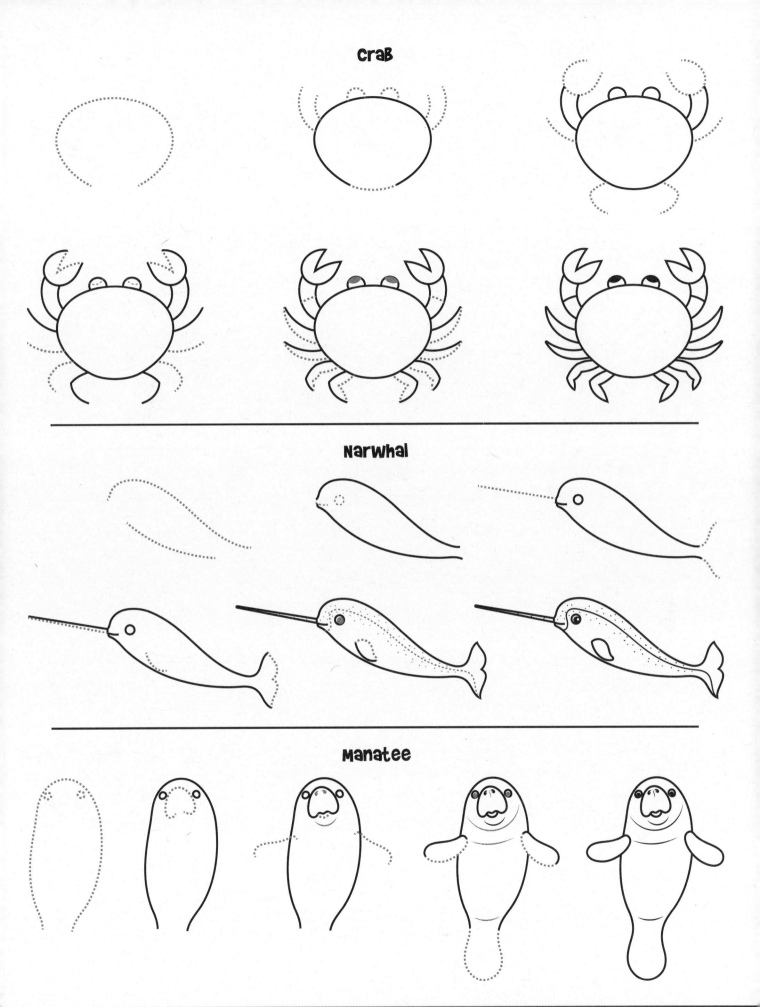

Narwhal

Manatee

Sea Turtle

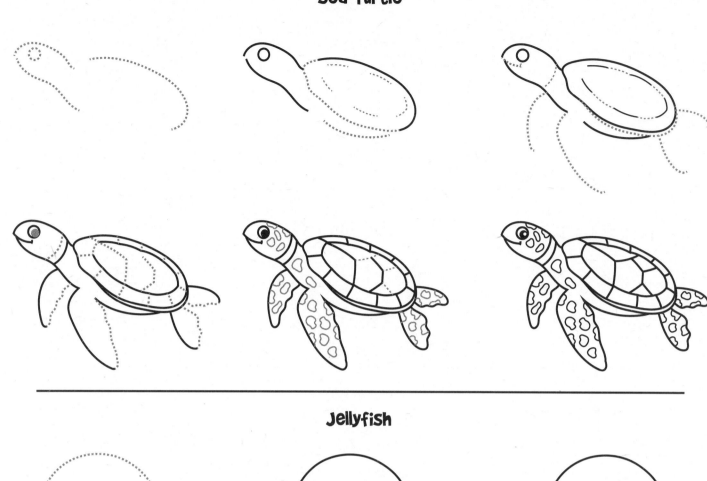

Jellyfish

Betta

Oscar

Dolphin

Sockeye Salmon

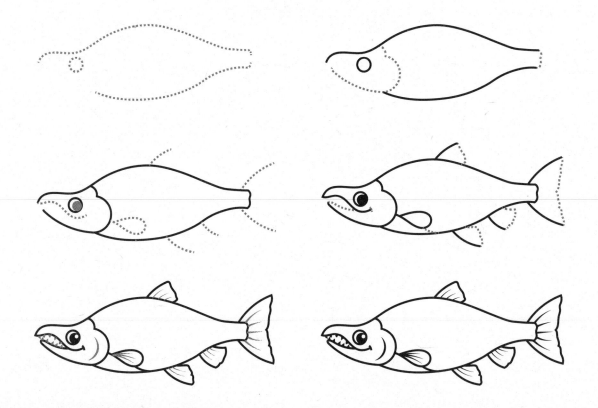

Tiger Shark

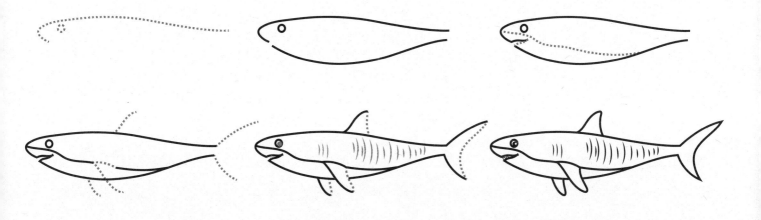

Pygmy Shark

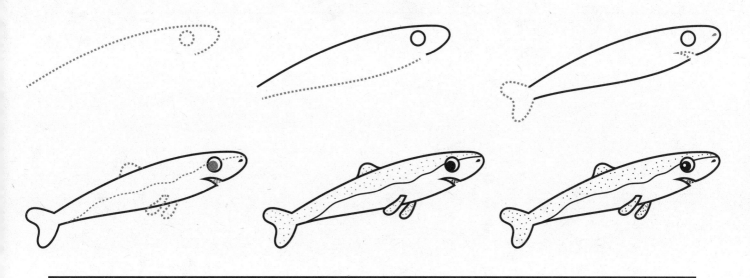

Great White Shark

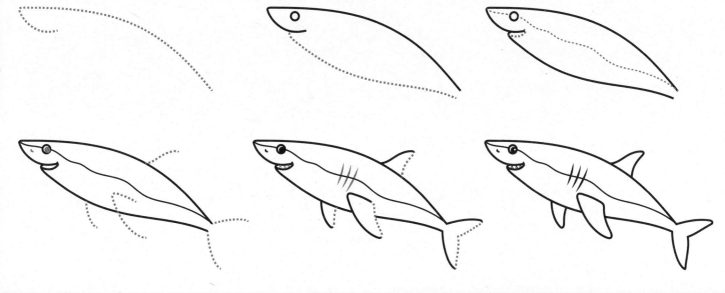

DISCUS

 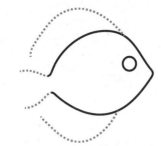 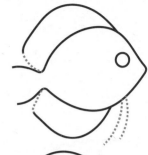

GUPPY

 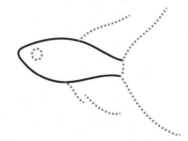 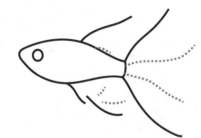

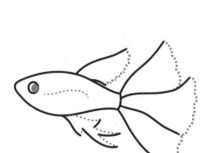 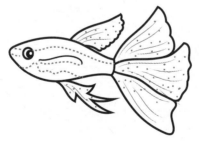 

Goldfish

 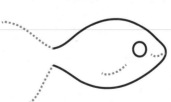 

Swordtail

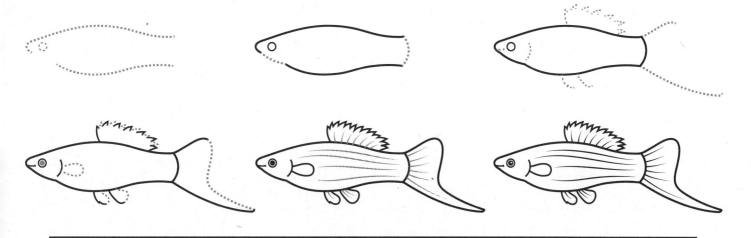

Neon Tetra

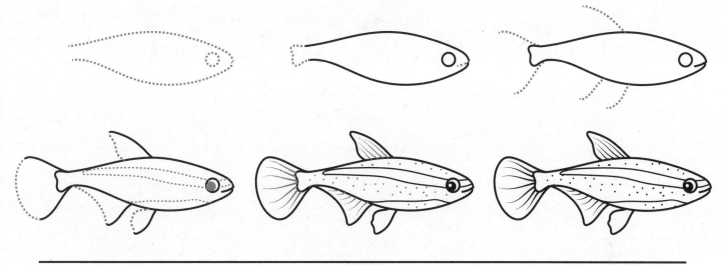

Molly

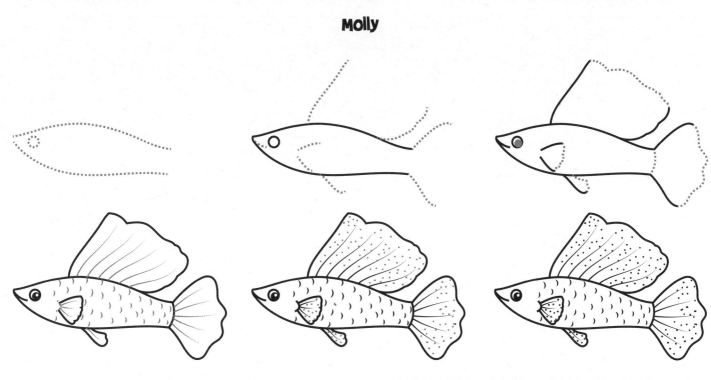

Walrus

Spotted Seal

Steller Sea Lion

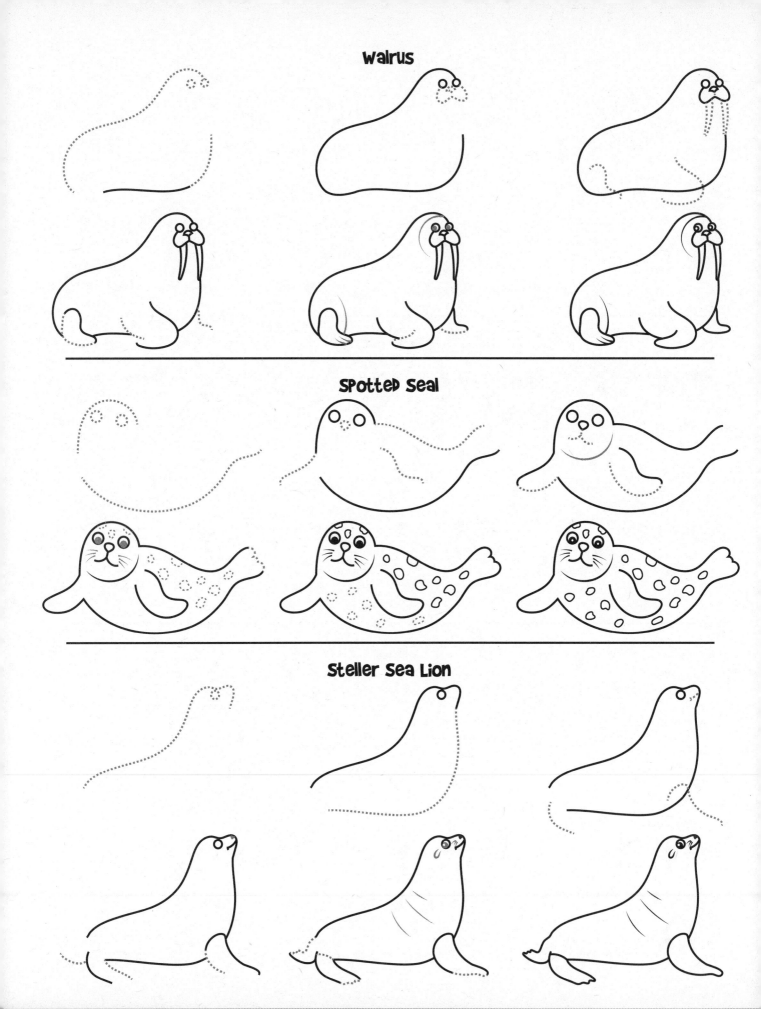

Striped Bass

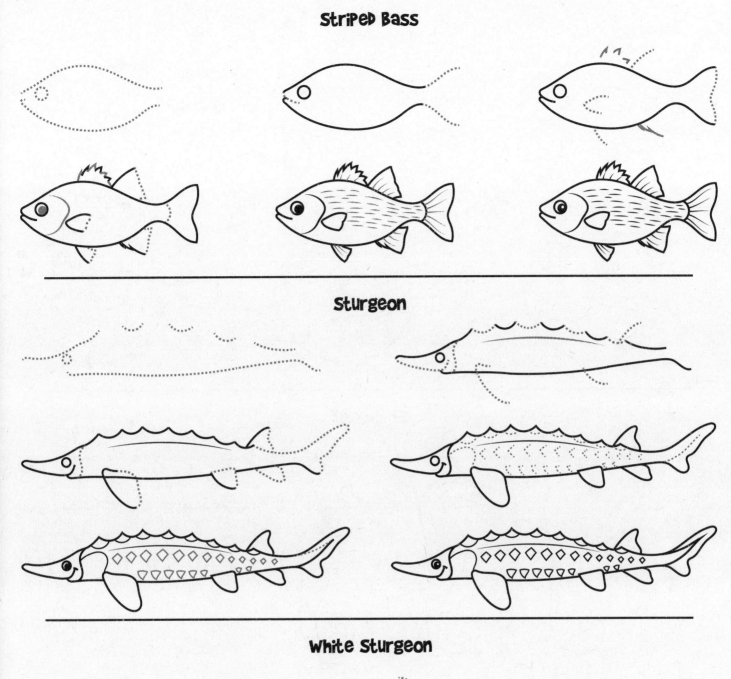

Sturgeon

White Sturgeon

Puffer fish

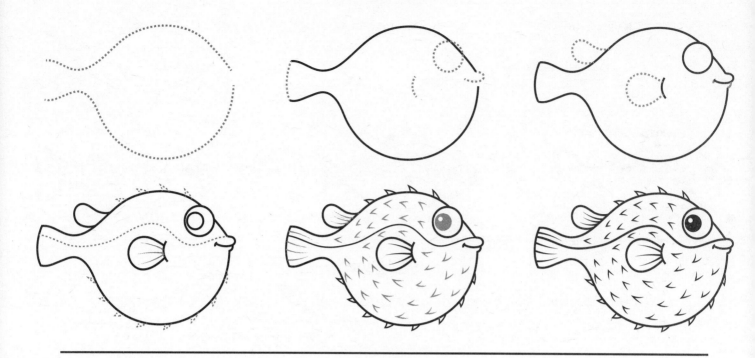

Seahorse

Trout

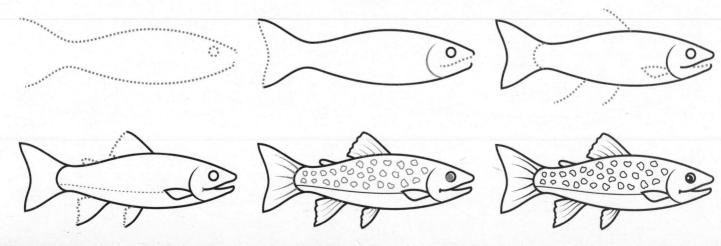

Hammerhead Shark

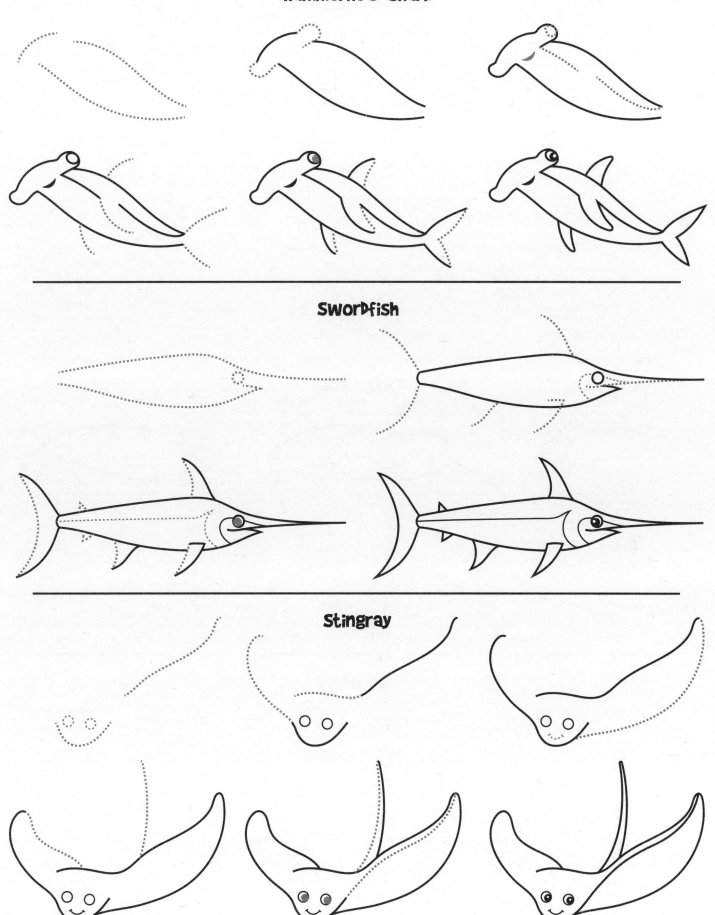

Swordfish

Stingray

Beluga Whale

Killer whale

Blue whale

LoBster

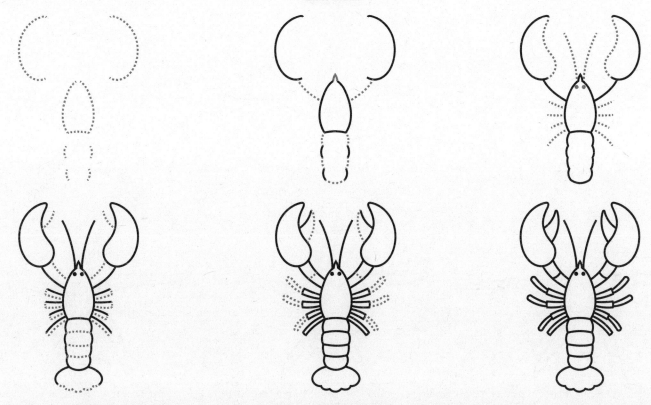

Royal Starfish

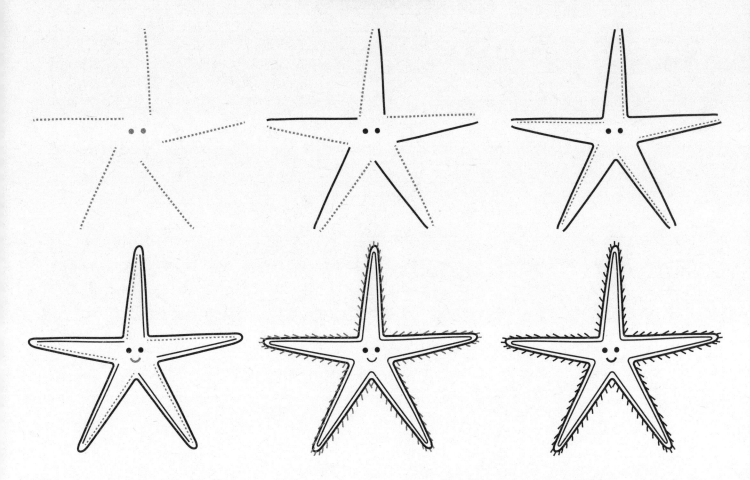

Egyptian Sea Star

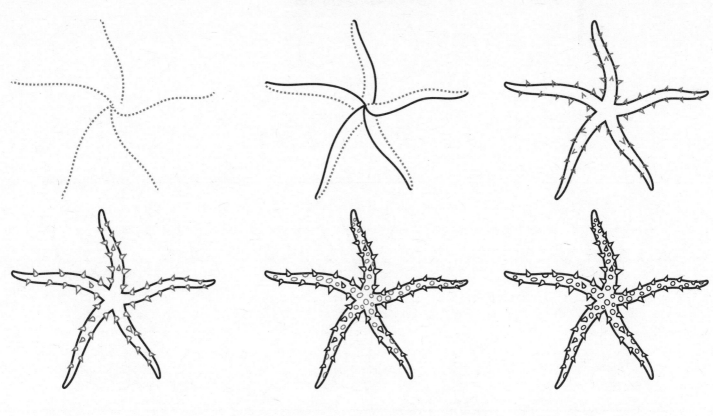

Australian Southern Sand Star

Dinosaurs & Extinct Animals

AlBertosaurus

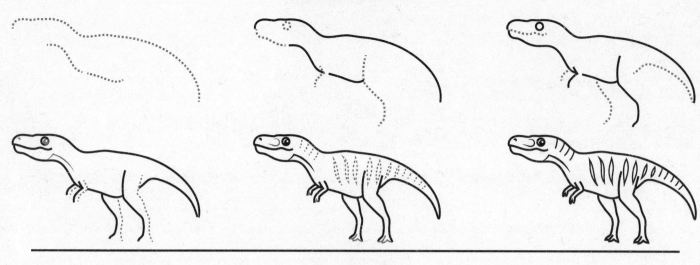

Ornithomimus

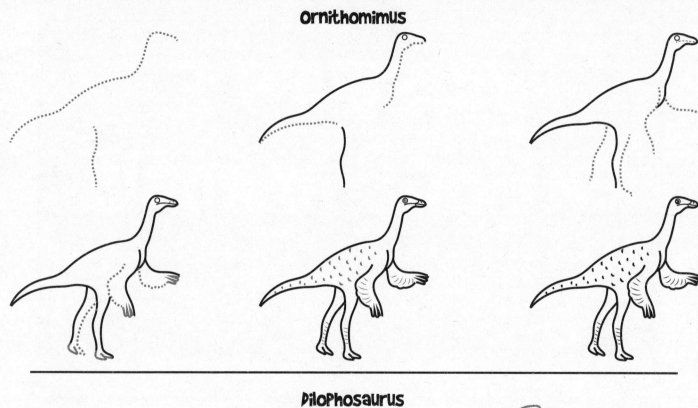

Dilophosaurus

Anchiceratops

Alectrosaurus

Allosaurus

Baryonyx

Apatosaurus

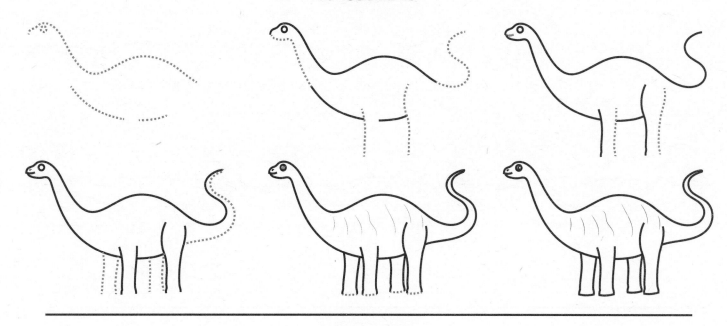

Ankylosaurus

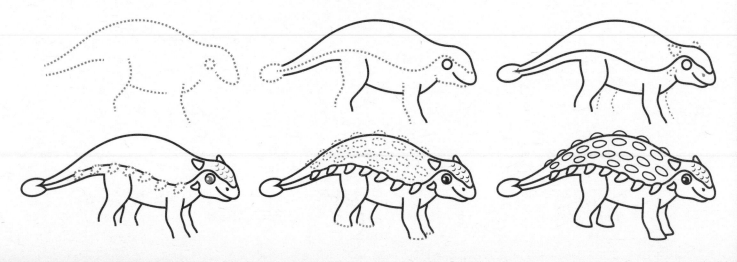

Corythosaurus

Deinonychus

Coelophysis

Pterosaur

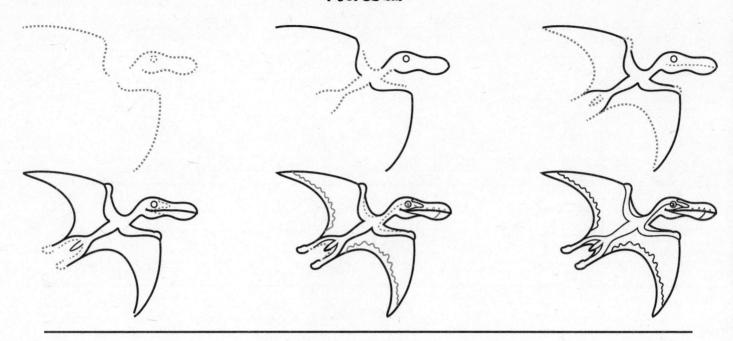

Mamenchisaurus

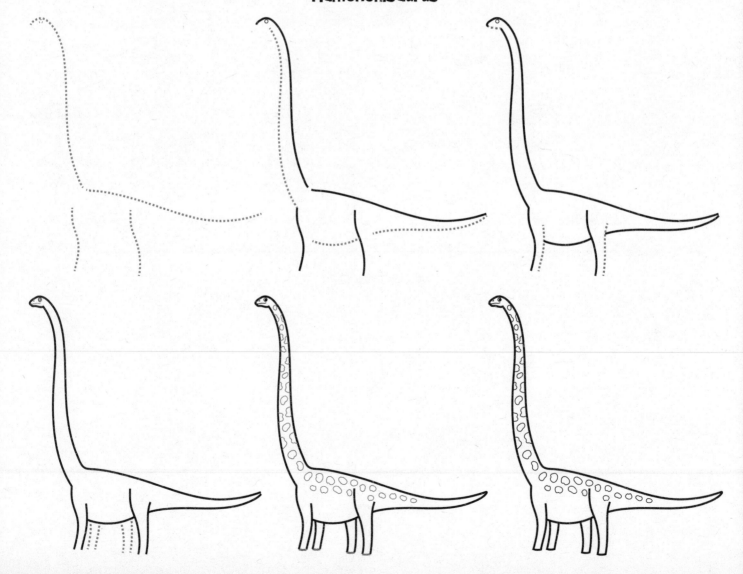

Iguanodon

Ichthyovenator

Hadrosaurus

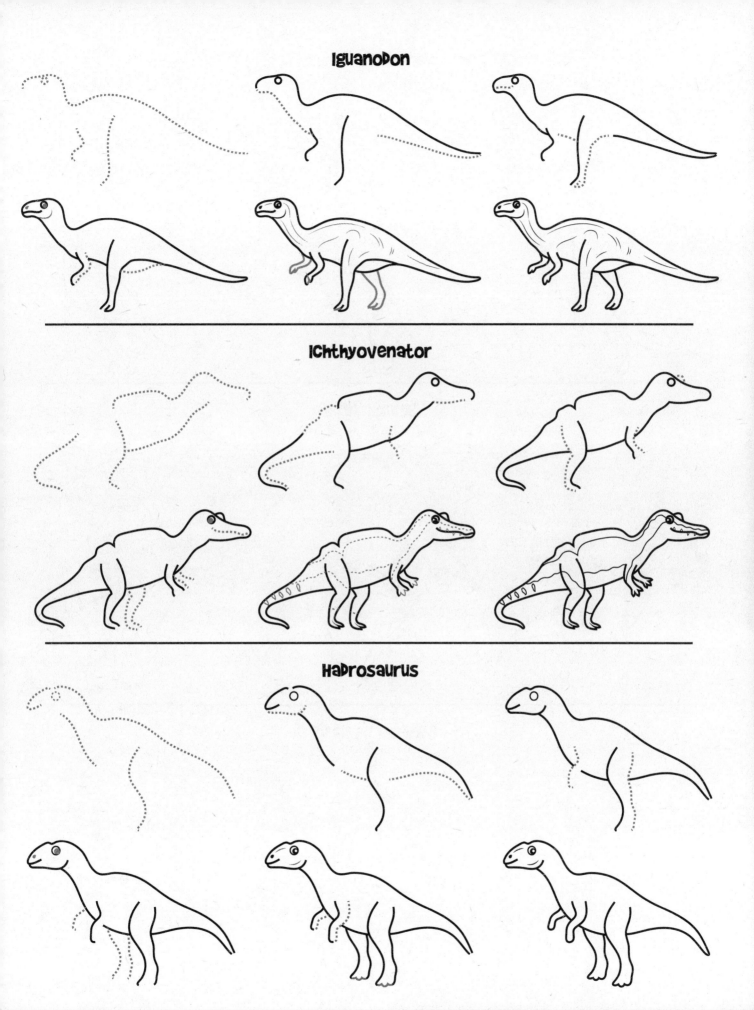

Parasaurolophus

Spinosaurus

KunBarrasaurus

Euoplocephalus

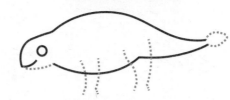
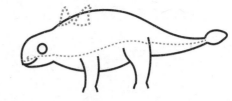

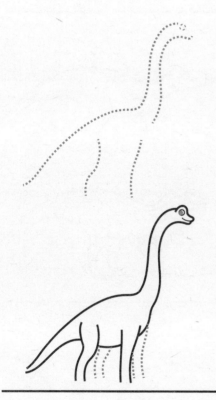
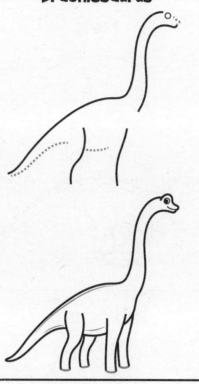
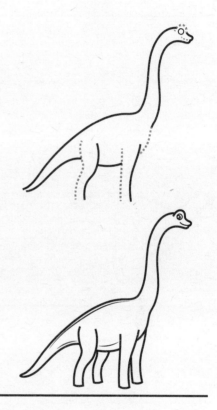

Brachiosaurus

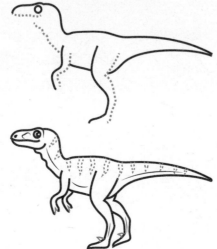
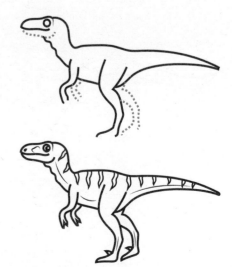

Velociraptor

Kentrosaurus

Dilong

Pleurosaurus

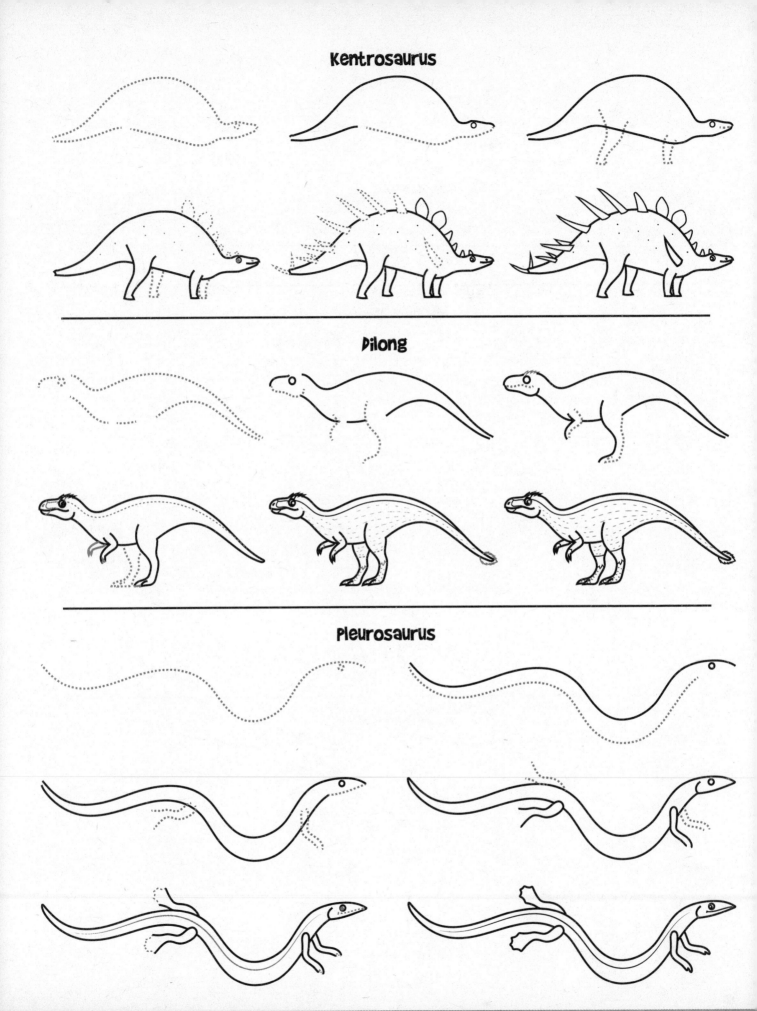

EDmontosaurus

Stegosaurus

LamBeosaurus

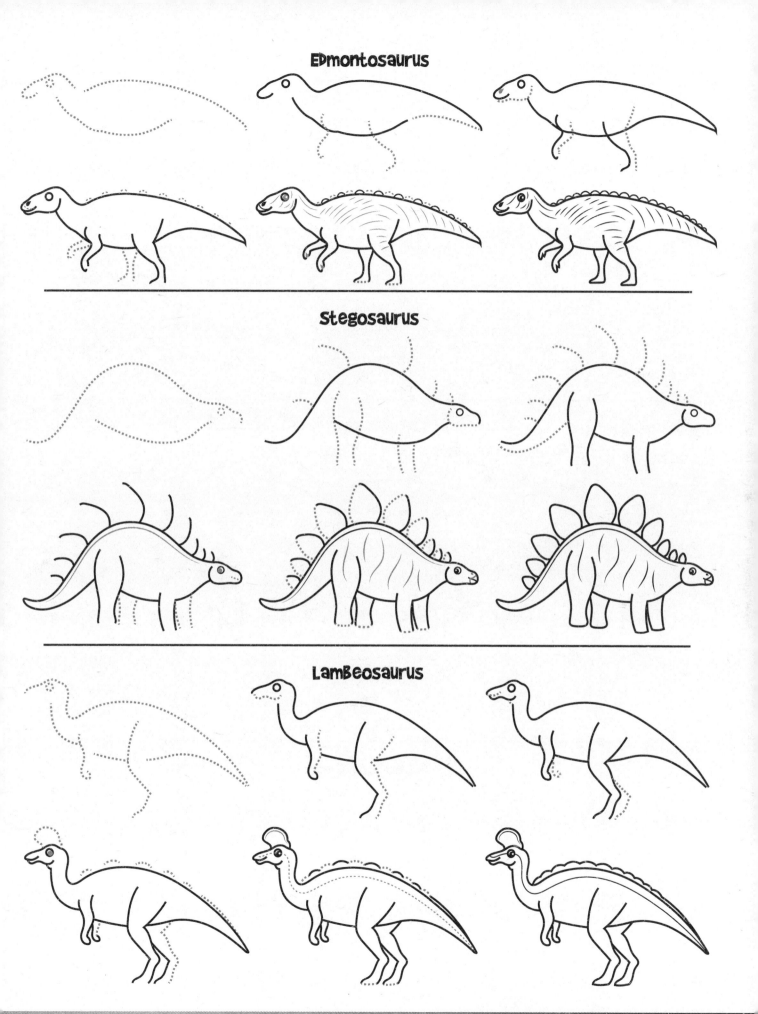

Struthiomimus

Lesothosaurus

Giganotosaurus

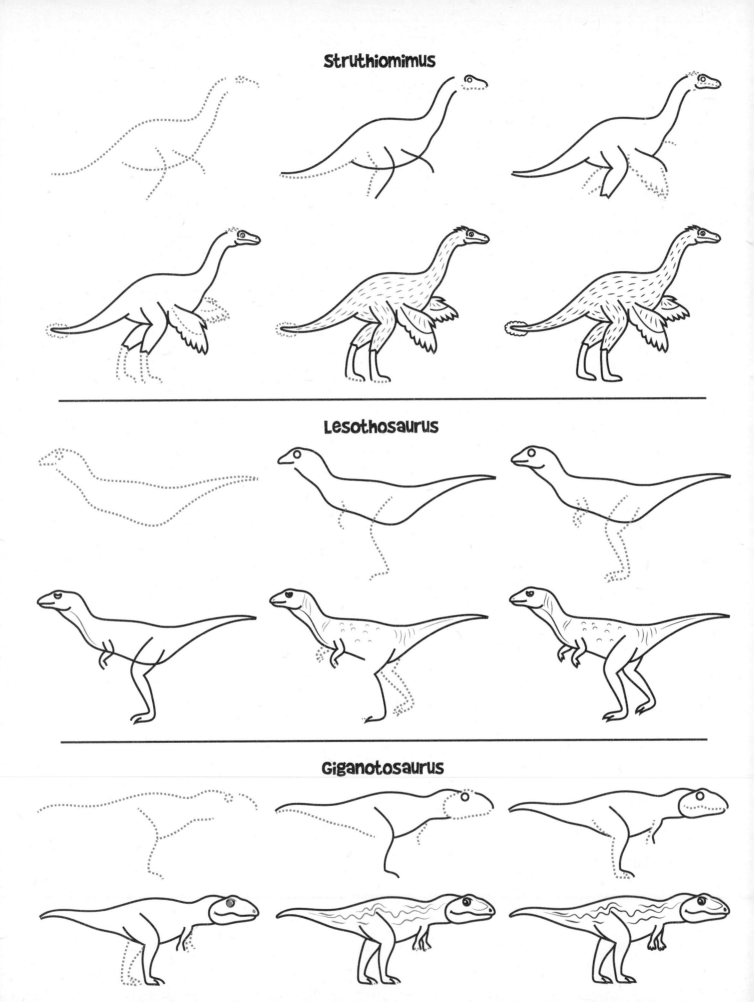

Tyrannosaurus Rex

Triceratops

Suchomimus

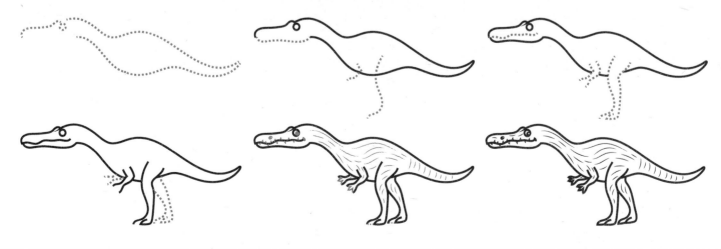

Passenger Pigeon

Dodo Bird

Great Auk

Dire Wolf

American Lion

Thylacine

Sabertooth Tiger

Wooly Mammoth

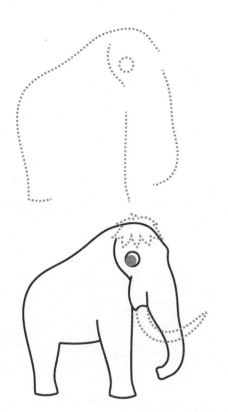
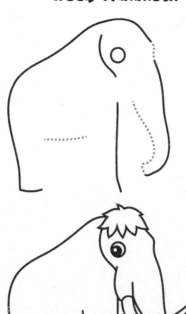

Paramylodon

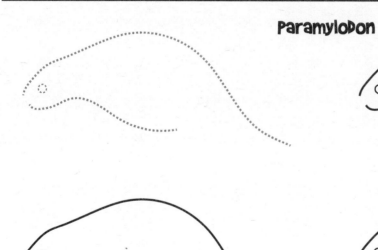

American Camel

Eastern Elk

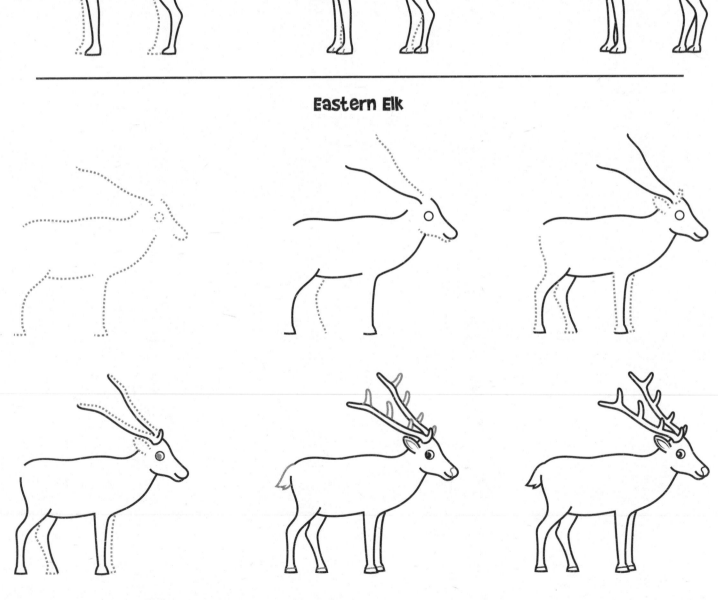

HyPohiPPus

Quagga

NEED some SPACE to PRACtiCE?
Give it a shot here!

Mythological Beasts

Phoenix

Unicorn

Peryton

Sphinx

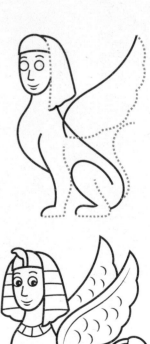

Manticore

Pegasus

Loch Ness Monster

Kraken

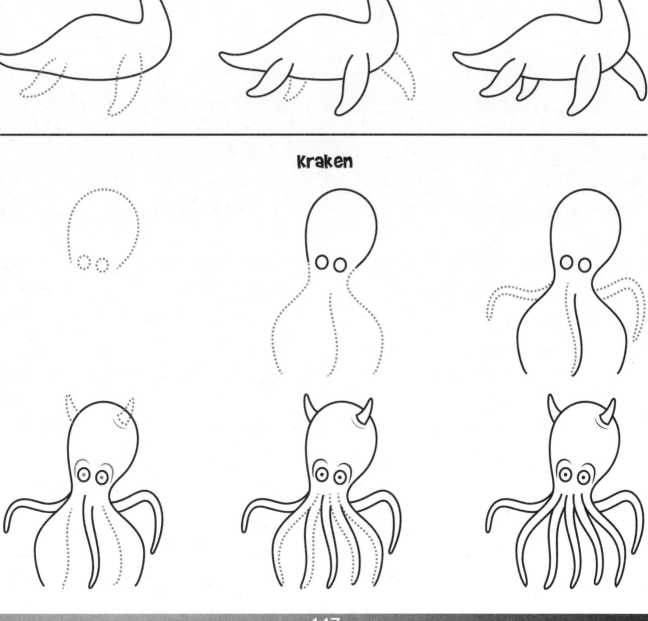

Jörmungandr

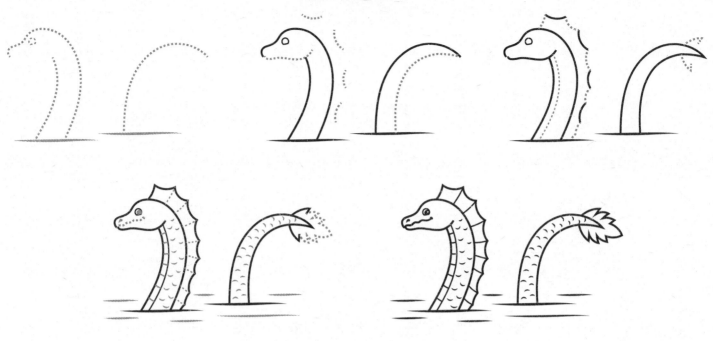

Kirin

HiPPoCampus

HiPPogriff

cockatrice

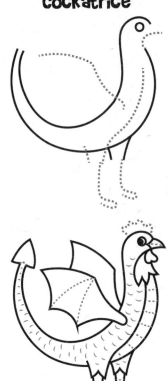

Griffin

Dragon, Eastern

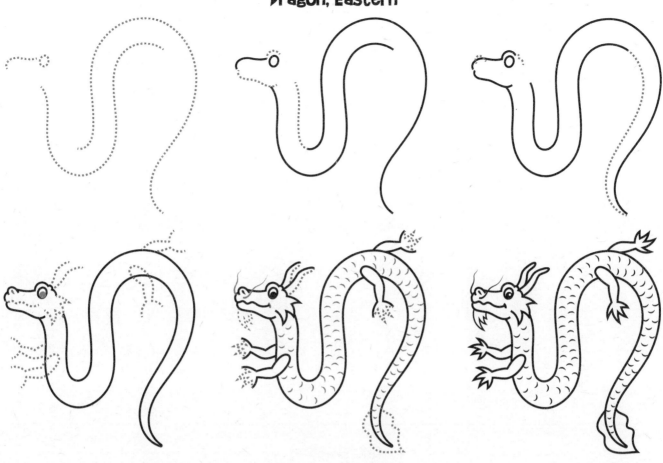

Dragon, Western

Chimera

Chupacabra

Basilisk

cerBerus

NEED some space to Practice?
Give it a shot here!

InDex

Mango Publishing, established in 2014, publishes an eclectic list of books by diverse authors—both new and established voices—on topics ranging from business, personal growth, women's empowerment, LGBTQ studies, health, and spirituality to history, popular culture, time management, decluttering, lifestyle, mental wellness, aging, and sustainable living. We were recently named 2019 and 2020's #1 fastest growing independent publisher by Publishers Weekly. Our success is driven by our main goal, which is to publish high quality books that will entertain readers as well as make a positive difference in their lives.

Our readers are our most important resource; we value your input, suggestions, and ideas. We'd love to hear from you—after all, we are publishing books for you!

Please stay in touch with us and follow us at:

Facebook: Mango Publishing

Twitter: @MangoPublishing

Instagram: @MangoPublishing

LinkedIn: Mango Publishing

Pinterest: Mango Publishing

Newsletter: mangopublishinggroup.com/newsletter

Join us on Mango's journey to reinvent publishing, one book at a time.

Woo! Jr. Kids' Activities is passionate about inspiring children to learn through imagination and FUN. That is why we have provided thousands of craft ideas, printables, and teacher resources to over 55 million people since 2008. We are on a mission to produce books that allow kids to build knowledge, express their talent, and grow into creative, compassionate human beings. Elementary education teachers, day care professionals, and parents have come to rely on Woo! Jr. for high quality, engaging, and innovative content that children LOVE. Our best-selling kids activity books have sold over 375,000 copies worldwide.

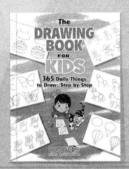    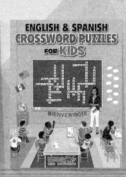 

Tap into our free kids activity ideas at our website WooJr.com or by following us on social media:

ⓟ https://www.pinterest.com/woojrkids/
ⓕ https://www.facebook.com/WooJr/
ⓨ https://twitter.com/woojrkids
ⓞ https://www.instagram.com/woojrkids/